VOW OF ALIVENESS

SAYING YES TO THE MESS AND MAGIC OF A TRUE LIFE

RAVI BAIKEI MISHRA

For Joshua, Gigi, Melissa, and other dear ones whose fire and intensity to live both lights the path forward and, on occasion, leaves burn scars (myself, as you will see, very much included)

CONTENTS

ZEN EVENING GATHA

Let me respectfully remind you
Life and death are of supreme importance
Time swiftly passes by, and opportunity is lost
Each of us should strive to awaken...
Awaken
Take heed, do not squander your life

INTRODUCTION: LET ME RESPECTFULLY REMIND YOU

It was my first night at Zen Mountain Monastery in 2016, and the bell had just rung, marking the end of the final meditation period that evening. The *zendo*, or meditation hall, was almost dark, with the last light of the sun poking through the narrow slit windows, dimly illuminating the trees outside. Stillness permeated every molecule around me, freezing time itself.

I didn't quite know what was going on. Every other time that the bell rang, everyone got up and began the next activity, whether it was walking meditation, a liturgical service, or leaving the meditation hall. But this time, nobody moved.

Then the *han*, a traditional wooden board used as an instrument, was struck, and the *kokyo*, or designated chanting leader, read the *Zen Evening Gatha*:

> *Let me respectfully remind you*
> *Life and death are of supreme importance*
> *Time swiftly passes by, and opportunity is lost*
> *Each of us should strive to awaken...*
> *Awaken*

Her voice cut through the silence — and through me. A chill ran up my spine, one that has been repeated most nights I've spent at the monastery since then.

Moments later, as the echoes from *"Do not squander your life"* faded away, I got up from my cushion, bowed to the Buddha on the altar along with the 40 or so people there, and quietly exited the *zendo*. I made my way up the hill to my cabin, still not quite sure what hit me.

The *Zen Evening Gatha* is chanted every night at meditation centers and monasteries around the globe. It's an exhortation to practice and wake up, to examine and open our minds and hearts while we're alive and have the opportunity to do so.

It doesn't tell us anything new. We've all seen time swiftly pass us by and felt the lost opportunities that sometimes come with it: the thing we didn't say, the project we didn't start, the love we didn't share, the chance we didn't take.

Each of us, in our own way, wants to be awake — wants to live life *alive*. We all have stuff that is important to us, stuff we want to prioritize as we go through life. We all want to appreciate the little and big moments of pleasure, joy, and wonder that are all around us.

LIFE AND DEATH ARE OF SUPREME IMPORTANCE

According to the National Institute of Health (NIH), the #1 regret Americans have on their deathbed is, "I wish I lived a life true to myself, not the life others expected of me." On the surface, this seems almost silly. How can we *not* live a life true to ourselves? If they're not true to ourselves, who or what are our lives true *to*?

And yet I've spent whole chapters of my life — multiple years in a few cases — chasing success at work or dating a particular person while being driven, deep down, by how I wanted to look in the eyes of others. I created whole worlds within this motivation that have entangled not just myself but many people around me, like when I started a company and raised investment, only to realize, years later, that my heart wasn't all that into it.

Avoiding the life others expect of us is a surprisingly complicated thing. We're hardwired to want acceptance. It's one of our most basic drives. The incentives and dynamics of our culture and economic systems — which drive social approval, and often financial survival — powerfully pull us towards living according to others' expectations.

This pull is so powerful because it's *coming from within*. The behaviors, values, and patterns that we see prioritized around us shape the way we think and make meaning from experience. We need to understand how the background context of our lives reproduces itself within the logic of how we think, speak, and act if we are to "live a life true to ourselves."

Inspired by alternative communities that have adopted this term, I call this background context the "default world." The default world is populated by people, companies, and cultural forces that have an agenda, from social media apps and fashion influencers to corporate CEOs and politicians. Some of the time, these parties act for our benefit, but *all* of the time, they *want something from us* — a click, a like, a dollar, a vote.

Advertising is designed to make us feel unworthy. Food is scientifically created to get us addicted. Endless newsfeeds and autoplay videos are constantly sucking us into our screens. Across our entire lives, the default world is trying to control us to its own ends.

It runs on our attention, money, and impulsiveness. It tricks us into consumerism, status-seeking, and superficiality as forms of self-worth. It wages war on our self-esteem, mental health, and even our friendships. From the design of our food system to our addiction-inducing healthcare to social media to almost every single one of the countless ads we come across in modern life, our sense of truth, life, and depth is constantly under siege. Feeling whole, complete, and at ease — without needing to scroll, consume, and dissociate our way through life — is the blood enemy of the default world.

Just in case you were worried our predicament wasn't hard enough, I left out one small detail: *we* are the default world. We work at those companies, consume those products, and click and scroll countless times a day. We're not *trying* to harm ourselves or anyone else – we're just trying to get by and live our lives.

This is the knot we must untie. We must uproot our attachment to the default world if we are to live the simple truth that our life — our specific, personal, unique Aliveness — is of supreme importance.

TIME SWIFTLY PASSES BY, OPPORTUNITY IS LOST

The first stage of every Buddhist practice is raising *bodhicitta,* the intention to be awake and alive. *Bodhichitta* arises when we realize what's at stake in accepting the default world: *our lives.* If you're genuinely content in the default life, I take my hat off to you. This book will probably not be your cup of tea, and I admire your chill.

But my hunch is that this "chill" is simply the avoidance of fear. A true life is much harder, scarier, and more vulnerable than the life others expect of us — at least up until potentially regretting how we spent our days on our deathbed, that is.

Vow of Aliveness is about prioritizing what's important in our hearts despite the consequences. I will tell you about how I've centered Aliveness, but doing this has often led to heartbreak. Companies I started failed, relationships I threw all of myself into ended, and so often I had nothing to show for it. Fear of failure and the reality of rejection are just as much a part of Aliveness as joy and success. What distinguishes Aliveness is that however things go, we *engage* with our lives, exploring and expressing what matters most to us — and the soul-level satisfaction of doing this transcends our ideas about how we want our lives to go.

Aliveness comes from learning to hear and trust the whispers of our Inner World. The trick isn't to figure out where to go and what to do, but rather to stop drowning out the whispers. If we listen, they lead us home.

So before we begin, I ask you to raise *bodhichitta* — to connect with the Aliveness-seeking part of yourself. This is personal: What opportunities have you lost? Projects never started, hobbies unexplored, life loves you never got the courage to ask out?

How about today? Did you enjoy your breakfast, or was it scarfed down in front of a screen or running to some place you had to be? Are you feeling the passing of time as the beauty of the days of your life — or trying to ignore aging as an unconscious (or *very conscious*) fear of death? Are you more interested in squeezing, cajoling, and planning your life to get what you want or the here-and-now life energy flowing through your veins?

I believe we all have a voice and force inside of us yearning to live our deepest, truest life. Ultimately, this part needs to become so powerful that it transcends the fear, smallness, and seeming safety that keep us in cycles of living according to others' expectations. And in case you need a little extra motivation, don't forget: time swiftly passes by, and opportunity is lost.

EACH OF US SHOULD STRIVE TO AWAKEN

I came to write this book after leading workshops on life reflection and prioritization. My core method was simple: carve out time every quarter to reflect on what's important and brainstorm ways to actually do those things in everyday life. They seemed to help folks who showed up in a no-brainer, "Yeah, I should probably think about what's important regularly" sort of way.

But under the surface, I was drawing on almost two decades of Zen training and meditation practice. The exercises I shared were designed to help discover what's truly meaningful via presence and intuition. Simultaneously, they were rooted in practicality and a results-orientation that I had learned from leading software teams throughout my career. Using a variety of techniques, the workshops explored one core question: where in my life am I feeling most alive, and how can I tangibly nurture that Aliveness?

I found that people seemed to be getting a lot from them. It wasn't just my friends showing up, but friends of folks who had previously shown up and random strangers on the internet who had somehow found my writing.

These people wanted to know more about my methods, and, more personally, I wanted to articulate them in greater depth. As I started writing, I realized that the complete story of these workshops needed to include not just the exercises and philosophies but also the pieces of myself and my past that they came from. The result is the book you're holding: a mix between a memoir of navigating Zen training within a modern, entrepreneurial, and activist life and a framework for prioritizing Aliveness amidst the default world.

AWAKEN

The start of this book would not be complete without a proper introduction. Hi. My name is Ravi Baikei Mishra. (Baikei is my *dharma* name within my Zen community, translating to "cultivating wisdom" — more on that later.) I'm an able-bodied Indian American man, born in Kanpur, India and raised in San Jose, California, the heart of Silicon Valley.

The dichotomy between these two places has shaped my core perspectives. In the Bay Area, I've been at the epicenter of one of the most transformative periods in human history and witnessed one of the largest explosions of wealth ever seen. I've taken for granted and then deeply questioned the idea that technology is uniformly good for humanity. I continue to believe that it can be a force for progress — but I'm increasingly skeptical of where it's headed within the economic systems of today.

Then there's India. In frequent short visits to see my family there while growing up and in longer, wandering, spiritually seeking trips as an adult, I've experienced some of the most tender, profound, and beautiful moments of my life. In simple activities like walking down crowded, smelly, noisy streets and taking showers out of a bucket, I've felt alive in ways I can hardly imagine in the U.S. In the process, I've seen how my experience of life is not as clearly linked to my material surroundings as I normally assume they are.

I carry both of these heritages with me — a Silicon Valley curiosity and optimism that things are changing for the better and an Indian spirituality that crackles with Aliveness amidst both simplicity and chaos.

My enthusiasm has led to a life that moves between worlds. I've founded startups and led product teams at some of the world's most cutting-edge tech companies. I've also joined activist movements and dedicated large portions of my life to social change work. From hanging out with Arab Spring revolutionaries in Cairo to spiritual practice in remote monasteries deep in the Himalayas, I've dedicated myself to understanding and exploring liberation within myself and across our world.

Alongside all of that, over the 17 years since I took a course on Zen Buddhism during my senior year of college, I've meditated basically every day, read countless books on Buddhism, and joined a Zen monastery (Zen Mountain Monastery, or ZMM for short, in upstate New York) where I currently spend a month each year to train with my teacher. I've done dozens of extended meditation retreats and thrown myself into Zen training with every fiber of my being. It's transformed my life and continues to do so every day.

I relish this intersectionality. It has shown me what Aliveness looks like in a variety of contexts — and taught me how I can prioritize it no matter where I am or what I'm doing. Most of all, it's allowed me to dream that all of us — whether we're living in a monastery, changing the world, or just trying to get by — can live life *alive*, can awaken.

TAKE HEED, DO NOT SQUANDER YOUR LIFE

The challenges, triumphs, and methods of living a life of Aliveness are the crux of this book. In the first part of it, Recognizing the Predicament, I'll share the starting points of my adult life:

Zen training, passion projects, relationships, and what all of it — from the highest highs to the lowest lows — was teaching me about being alive. Along the way, we'll explore the core messages of the default world and the myriad ways our culture and surroundings are set up to chip away at our inherent self-worth.

In Part 2, Yes to the Mess and Magic, I'll share how I started to understand the task of Aliveness within the default world, and where that realization led me: on a backpacking trip around the globe, deep into the heart of social movements, and, yes, another entrepreneurial project. I'll plumb the depths of life today and the forces of the default world that separate us from our true life: distraction, dissociation, busyness, anxiety, numbness, and more.

Using the psychology of habit formation, we'll explore how some of these blockers take form in habit loops. These loops gain power over not just how we use our time and energy but how we understand who we are. If we are to live authentically *alive*, we must overthrow these habit loops, both inside our heads and in how we live our lives.

I'll share my journey of trying to do this, contextualizing it within Zen training and teaching. I'll explore how Zen has kept me connected with what's bringing me to life and given me the inner trust to prioritize it in how I live. I'll share why, given the inescapable nature of the default world, my journey of Aliveness has turned into a vow — and what that vow means for my life.

Part 3 of the book, The Loop of Aliveness, offers a framework for cultivating Aliveness with a few essential ingredients: curiosity, embodiment, charge, and allowing. We'll explore what these mean, how they're practiced, and the potential they carry to transform our lives. The Loop offers us a path to reclaim our power, to slowly but surely reverse the default world conditioning that wears away our connection with ourselves.

Finally, in Part 4, Living the Vow, I'll share the ways I bring this Loop to life. Knowing how easy it is to fall into the clutches of the default world and its mindsets, I've filled my life with rituals, practices, and communities that support my Aliveness. All of these are rooted in making it easier to choose the Loop in the big and small moments of my life.

First, I hold my life within the context of life prioritization rituals, which I shared a little about above. In that quarterly gathering and in a bite-sized way every day, I lean on presence to guide what I give my energy to.

Second, I'll present practices for expanding our capacity for Aliveness and presence *off* of the meditation cushion and across our lives. Hopefully, the somewhat quirky list of exercises in this chapter sparks ideas for how you can do the same.

Third, I'll tell you about the life-giving alternative spaces that are my refuge from the default world. Some of these are immersive and require travel, spanning from my Zen monastery to festivals like Burning Man. But perhaps the most important are the regular gatherings and communities right where we live — and I'll share how we can find and commit to these in our everyday lives.

I'll end with a note on how we can collaborate to nourish our collective Aliveness. Our world needs our Aliveness as much as we individually do. I yearn for ways we can both nourish our lives and bring sanity, beauty, and transformation into our communities and society.

One last note: throughout the book, I'll capitalize a few words, most notably Aliveness and Inner World. Aliveness is the experience of being present while following what genuinely brings us to life. It's both the simple peace of inhabiting our bodies right now and the active engagement with what deeply matters to us.

The stuff that "deeply matters to us" does so because it resonates with our Inner World, the unique universe within each of us that makes us who we are. Our Inner World is the source of our Aliveness, and our connection with it leads us to our true life. I did not create these terms, but capitalizing both of them is meant to denote and symbolize their sacredness and mystery.

Thanks for being here. May we all take heed, and not squander our lives.

PART I

RECOGNIZING THE PREDICAMENT

If I didn't define myself for myself, I would be crunched into other people's fantasies for me and eaten alive.

Audre Lord

✻

It is no measure of health to be well-adjusted to a profoundly sick society.

Jiddu Krishnamurti

✻

We live in a world where we have to hide to make love, while violence is practiced in broad daylight.

John Lennon

1

STARTING AT THE BEGINNING

"I REALLY WISH we had a very, very loud megaphone," I said. I lined up a strike and kicked the ball towards the net, but my friend saved it. The year was 2007, the place was San Jose, California, and I was at a neighborhood park playing soccer with one of my best friends, Saahil, while home from college on summer break. We casually kicked around the ball, with Saahil (who played for his university's soccer team) interspersing juggling tricks between passes. (Show off.) In that distinctly boys-wanting-to-play-sports way, we were bored.

"It'd be easier than knocking on doors! There's gotta be other kids on break, I bet we could get a dozen people to show up for a pickup game. We might blow out a few eardrums in the process, but, you know, it'd be worth it."

We laughed. But slowly, we looked at each other, a dawning realization hitting us both simultaneously. Facebook had recently launched, and we were starting to understand the organizing power of online social networks. We didn't need a loud megaphone — we just needed a way to gather people who wanted to play. Maybe there was a way for us to do this by building something on the internet.

That simple reflection would turn into my work for the next 5 years of my life.

In the days that followed, I dove into how, when, and where people play sports casually. I realized that while pickup games were widespread, organized sports leagues were even more popular — and, well, not very organized. Most leagues used paper sign-up forms and aggregated participant information in spreadsheets. They struggled to reach potential players and to get them to sign up.

I saw these problems at my college, the University of Pennsylvania, where I played various sports in the school-organized intramural leagues. For example, we needed to write out our credit card numbers on paper forms to register, which seemed like an unnecessary security risk. Often, we wouldn't know which fields or courts our games were scheduled to be played on or if a game was canceled because of the rain.

It was clear to me that these leagues would be run very differently within a few years, and I wanted to build this future. I found an engineering lead and co-founder, Bo, from an MIT alumni email list. Together, we began creating a league management software product we named Athleague. In September 2007, we raised $300,000 from angel investors to help us get the company off the ground.

When I got back to college that month, schoolwork took a back seat. I spent my days building Athleague and selling our pilot product to universities. By the end of the semester, we had a working prototype, and I'd called hundreds of schools around the country.

It was delightful work, and I was on cloud nine. Growing up in Silicon Valley, I had wanted to start a company since I was a kid, and here I was, fulfilling that dream before I even graduated from college. Even better, the thing I was building

4

would help more people play sports, one of my deepest loves at the time. As 2007 turned to 2008, I cruised into my last semester in college, excitedly building my dream project and living a life full of passion, friends, and fun.

ENCOUNTERING ZEN

It was at this blissful time, in January 2008, that I found myself taking a class that would transform my life. I had to fulfill a few last requirements to graduate, and when I saw "Intro to Zen Buddhism" in the course catalog, I was instantly intrigued.

I knew Buddhism had its roots in Indian spirituality. Growing up, I read and watched adaptations of the *Mahabharata* and *Ramayana,* ancient epics that loom large in Indian culture. I had found myself attracted to the vibe of the meditating sages that showed up throughout the two stories. They exuded a sense of peace and inner knowing that seemed to flow from deep within their being. They clearly understood something essential about the nature of life, and it seemed meditation was the key to establishing this clarity.

But as I navigated growing up as an immigrant, I buried my fascination. Indian things were mostly absent in pop culture, but when they were there, the messages about them were consistent: Indian food was smelly, Indian accents were funny, and Indian people were nerdy. By the time I was a teenager, I wanted nothing to do with Indian culture.

Zen, however, was both not Indian and, it seemed, culturally cool. I remembered hearing famed Chicago Bulls coach Phil Jackson (of the Michael Jordan teams) referred to as the "Zen Master." From sports to business, successful people mentioned Zen in reverent tones. The class seemed like an interesting way to explore meditation, and I quickly signed up. On the first day of class, the professor offered three simple rules for the course:

"First, I'm going to teach you what Zen says about the nature of reality and who you are.

"Second, I'm going to ask you to meditate. I can't force you to do this, but to take this class and not meditate would be like taking a class on riding a bike and not actually riding a bike.

"Finally, I'm going to evaluate you based on a journal you keep. All I want you to do is write about how Zen teachings show up in your life. You could say they're all garbage, and that would be fine if that's really your experience."

I wasn't sure how seriously I was going to take the whole thing, but near the end of January, I found myself in the library late one night with a friend from class. He mentioned he had been raised by two Buddhist parents, and it showed. He moved unhurriedly, spoke deliberately, and maintained light but steady eye contact. It was connective and almost unnerving.

With a wry, cheeky smile, he leaned in and asked, "Want to meditate for twenty minutes?" Without thinking, I nodded, following him back to a spot that he said was his favorite. He produced two cushions seemingly from thin air, and right there, amidst the stacks in the back hallways of Van Pelt Library, we sat down.

He shared the practice instructions we had been given in the class: feel the body breathe, and when you notice your attention has gone elsewhere, return to the breath. He gave me a wink, said, "Good luck," and started the timer.

MY FIRST MEDITATION

In a scene from the classic movie *The Matrix*, Neo, the protagonist played by Keanu Reeves, gets his body hooked into a futuristic computer that allows him to learn every martial arts discipline in a few minutes.

Before he starts, he sees the screen in front of him and wonders, incredulously, "Jiu-Jitsu? I'm going to learn Jiu Jitsu?" The operator running the download smirks and starts the process.

The soundtrack plays a screeching electronic noise, and Neo's body shakes violently. A few moments later, the download ends, and Neo emerges.

"Holy shit."

The operator slyly responds, "Hey Mikey, I think he likes it." (For those too young to remember, this is a line from an old Life Cereal commercial.)

"How about some more?"

"Hell yeah!" Neo responds.

"Hell yeah" is the best way to describe that first meditation session. My body tingled with electricity even as my mind moved a million miles an hour. I replayed a dinner conversation with a friend, and a single word that friend said during the meal evoked a memory of playing sports as a teenager, and all of a sudden, I was in high school, running and catching a football on a crisp fall day — all in the span of what felt like 10 seconds. My hands glowed with a warmth I had never experienced. The sheer amount of mental territory covered and quality of sensory experience was, well, mind-blowing.

I felt the miraculous interconnection of the breath, a dramatic air-rushing-through-nose, belly-expanding, lungs-growing, entire-being-filling overwhelming all-at-onceness. It was like I had stepped into the path of a firehose: thoughts, emotions, sensations, and, most of all, *pure energy* flowed through me. As my mind settled, this firehose of energy slowly transformed into a ballet, each breath a wondrous symphony of muscles, blood, air, and space. In a "you never forget your first time" way, I caught a glimpse of the universe that was inside me.

It mostly wasn't quiet or peaceful — it was closer to the experience of a rock concert, but that didn't bother me in the slightest. Because meditation wasn't really popular back then, I wasn't carrying ideas of what it was supposed to feel like. I had no idea that so much was happening inside of me, and all I knew was that I, like Neo, wanted more.

Within a couple weeks, I was hooked. The combination of meditating, learning about Zen, and then exploring its teachings in the context of my life gave permission to immerse myself in my sensory experience in a way I never had before. I remember once I sat down to meditate and there was a piece of lint on the floor in front of me. I stared at it for half an hour, feeling my visual field fluctuate from crisp to wavy. I didn't know if it was "meditation" or not, and I didn't care.

For the rest of the semester, I meditated, reflected, and journaled — and my entire life began to transform. Whether I was eating a meal, listening to music, or making love with my girlfriend, it felt like someone had turned up the volume on my sensory experiences. Did the crisp and sweetness of an apple always dance on my tongue like this?

The answer was no — or, rather, that I could easily miss it. The exact same apple could *also* taste pedestrian and uninteresting — it completely depended on the quality of my awareness and my emotional state. These were the central intermediaries between myself and my life, and meditation was like cleaning the lens, letting me experience my world more vividly.

WHAT IS LOVE?

I need to take you back a few months because while Zen is at the core of this book, there was one teensy tiny thing I've been leaving out — one thing that was coursing through me with the force of a supernova. The greatest power in the universe, it's been called: love.

In early October 2007, the acapella/comedy troupe I was part of was invited to a show at a nearby university. I was excited, and not just because these trips were usually an absolute blast.

I had a crush on a young woman, Clara, who attended that college. We met the previous year and had kept in touch (via AOL Instant Messenger or AIM, as we did in those days). When I messaged her that I would be visiting, she seemed excited to come to the show, and my ever-optimistic mind took that as a good sign.

I wish I could share the details of how things went that night, but at this point, all I remember is engaging conversation, effortless dancing, and lingering eye contact. I can close my eyes and still feel the irresistible pull of our instant chemistry, the shimmer and sparkle that the memory shines with in my mind. I visited her the following weekend on fall break, and pretty soon, we were dating.

It was first love for us both, and we were smitten. She was brilliant, beautiful, and perhaps the most charismatic person I'd ever met. She said what was on her mind but did it with kindness and invitation, opening my mind with her perspectives on life, history, and science. Most of all, she was *open to life*, to going with the flow of whatever was happening. We were watching a horror movie once, and in a climactic moment, she non-ironically exclaimed, "Oh my god, I can't breathe. Awesome."

Her embrace of *everything* was infectious. She pulled me out of my head and into a vastness of the world that I had never known. The speed with which I fell in love seemed natural, even obvious. It wasn't even just me thinking she was incredible — pretty soon, my friends began pestering me about when she'd be visiting next so we could all hang out.

One afternoon, as we were on a walk, she sang me Alanis Morissette's love song, *Head Over Feet*. (The chorus refrain, *"you've already won me over, in spite of me,"* was a major theme for her within our relationship.) One of the lines — *I've never felt this healthy before / I've never wanted something rational —* has stuck with me as a helpful measuring stick for how relationships should feel. I had dated before but until then, nothing had ever felt this *healthy*. By the time I started the class on Zen in January 2008, we were deeply in love — the kind of love that was so on fire with life that everyone in the room felt it.

More broadly, I was *in love with my life*. I think this is why Zen stuck for me so completely: from work to friends to this magical relationship, life was amazing, and meditation was allowing me to savor it at a level I had never before.

ZEN, LOVE, AND ATTACHMENT

A word with Sanskrit roots, Buddhism literally translates to "Awake-ism." In Buddhist teaching, the central blocker to waking up to our Aliveness is *tanha*, craving or thirst. We suffer because we want stuff we don't have, or we don't want stuff that's happening to us (like getting old). This craving keeps us in a perpetual state of desire, longing, or attachment. We're unable to relax, enjoy, and fully experience the life that's happening right now.

One day in class, our professor related the story of a modern Zen scholar, DT Suzuki, as he was crying when his wife died. Someone asked him why he cried. If he was truly beyond attachment, death should not cause him sorrow, right?

As Suziki sobbed, he responded, "My tears have no roots." Our professor added some color: "When love is felt, just feel it completely. When it leads to sadness, be the sadness. There is no scheming around tragedy; non-attachment can't be forced. Eventually, love reveals itself as a process of letting go."

Woah. I still remember sitting up straighter in class when I heard those words. What did Suzuki mean? He was in love. He was sobbing at his wife's funeral. And yet his tears didn't have roots?

I'm in love too, I thought to myself, *but was my love a "process of letting go?"* If my relationship with Clara were to end, would my tears have roots? Does my *love* have roots? What did "roots" even mean? How could I love with all my heart and yet do so without attachment?

I brought this inquiry into my life. One evening in February 2008, Clara and I were returning home from dinner with a few of our friends while visiting her family. We were a few miles from where we were staying, and because she'd had a couple of drinks, it was on me to get us home. Here's what I wrote in my Zen journal about what happened next:

"I got in the car, but there was one problem: Clara's car was a stick shift, which I didn't know how to drive. Don't worry, she assured me, she would teach me while we drove back.

"The ride was nerve-racking, but despite stalling out time after time while driving on a main road, she remained patient and unnerved. More than that, though, she was so... tender. There was more care and affection in her voice than I had ever experienced, than I could possibly put into words. I've never felt a deeper moment of love and being loved in my whole life — and in that moment, I could feel there was no past, no future. Just this moment of now, of pure love."

It was the deepest love I had ever felt — but also I was scared. *"What will happen in a few months when I graduate?"* I wrote. *"I want to freeze this moment in time, make it last forever — even though I know that's not possible."*

BRINGING ZEN INTO MY LIFE

I was *in it*, exploring Zen teachings in a profound and personal way, alive with the fire and beauty I was feeling. The core of this exploration was sitting in daily meditation (or *zazen*, literally "sitting Zen"), which I did for 15-30 minutes a day throughout the semester.

Our professor consistently implored us to make *zazen* a priority. The heart of Zen teachings were not in the ideas presented; instead, they were truths to be experienced, and meditation was the key to unlocking them.

This method of exploration was a complete 180 from everything I'd ever learned. Usually, we're taught in words, numbers, and images, which are then put together in the form of ideas. Learning something usually meant understanding certain ideas and being able to apply them in appropriate contexts.

In Zen, there wasn't a pre-set, fixed thing to "learn." Instead, I was learning a way of living, exploring my reality with my body and heart rather than my head. Sitting (a word I'll use interchangeably with "meditating") was teaching me how to do this — how to keep it simple and just come back to the breath, back to this moment of life.

As I practiced, I began to notice *life* everywhere. Like the drive home with Clara, moments of love or wonder or joy burst forth spontaneously and consumed all of me. Eyes meeting, hands holding, the wind blowing through my hair, the clouds on a random morning. Zen training was teaching me to recognize and enjoy these moments as deeply as I could, without trying to hold on to them and make them last forever. For the first time, I was consciously touching the power of presence.

As I read the books on Zen assigned in class, I started to understand how Zen training grew outward from sitting meditation practice, creating ways to access and cultivate presence in the regular activities of life, like cooking, cleaning, and walking. Sauntering down Locust Walk (the main walking path through campus) one afternoon, I brought my attention to all the sounds I was hearing: leaves rustling, birds chirping, dozens of voices, laughter, the occasional shouts from student groups broadcasting their upcoming events.

Was there always this much going on? How was I normally missing so much of what was happening around me? Beforehand, I would have figured that hearing everything going on with such clarity would be annoying or stressful.

What I found was just the opposite — when I was listening without adding a commentary on top, my body felt at ease amidst the whole soundscape. The rest of the semester continued in this way — revelation after revelation about how enlivening it was to experience everything from deep love to simple activities with presence.

But graduation was looming. In May, my time in college ended. I moved back home to California to live with my parents while working out what would come next. The plan was to move to Boston, where my company's co-founder and the rest of our team were. It would be tough, but I figured Clara and I could make a long-distance relationship work. We had to try, knowing we couldn't just end something so amazing.

But as summer crept into fall, the market crashed. Just a few months prior, we were dreaming about a fundraising round to take our company to the next level. By October, we had to cut salaries in half to preserve cash.

On the relationship front, things started to fragment as Clara and I dealt with the reality of being on different coasts. On a visit to see Clara around that time, we started to confront some uncomfortable truths. She was still in college, and while our relationship had been incredible, even if I moved to Boston, we'd still be far apart geographically. Neither of us wanted to do a long-distance relationship for multiple years. With heavy hearts, we decided to break up.

By fall 2008, I was living in my childhood room, heartbroken from the end of this first, magical relationship and feverishly working out of my parent's garage, trying to turn things around for my startup.

2

ON BREAKUPS AND BREAKTHROUGHS

IT WAS time to deal with my new reality. I knew Clara and I had to part ways, but that didn't make it any less crushing. In an email she sent a few days later, she described her post-breakup subway trip home as "misery mixed with a Kundera acid trip metro ride," which just about summed it up for me as well.

We exchanged a few emails about how we were feeling, and in a later note on the same thread, I described how I had recently seen a documentary about climate change, an issue that Clara had helped me understand the importance of. In the post-breakup emotional exhaustion, I told her that I noticed I was feeling jaded about the issue. I wrote:

"I was watching this documentary and I could feel how I just didn't care about climate change. I wanted to push it away — screw it all, screw everything.

Then I realized what I was doing: rejecting you, something that made me think of you, a piece of what you meant to me. And I decided that's not going to be my approach — I'm going to cherish and internalize what you've taught me. I'm going to make sure our relationship, even if it's ended, adds to me and who I am rather than taking something away."

(Wow. I had a memory of writing something like this, but it was pretty wild to go back to the email thread and read my 22-year-old self express this sentiment so clearly. Also, I want to think I've grown out of my corny earnestness. My friends assure me I very much have not.)

And I wasn't just talking about climate change or a particular political orientation. Clara had opened my eyes and changed my life in more ways than I could ever describe (or even know). She taught me how to live with a profound simplicity and directness. When we sat down to eat, she would close her eyes and immerse herself in the first few bites of her meal, savoring whatever was in front of us. When we listened to music, she would softly sing along, her voice dancing with emotion and life. Without any relationship to Zen or Buddhism or any of the ideas and teachings that were becoming so central to who I was, she was a living, breathing representation of what it meant to be completely, ecstatically alive.

She was my first love, and I missed her.

But even just days after the breakup, I felt an emerging truth: this whole thing wasn't just about her. While the sadness was vast, I could sense an equally profound opportunity in my situation: realizing that her essence was still with me, within the Aliveness that lived *inside me.*

She lived expansive, curious, *authentic* — she was totally herself. In being so, she opened up space for me to be more and more *myself* — a process that didn't need to stop now that I was single. Every experience I had felt with her resulted from sensations and biochemicals coursing through *my own body*. I, too, could close my eyes and savor the first few bites of a meal. I could lie in bed and lose myself in the beauty of music.

And so I knew, somehow, that while I missed her, if I lived my life in a way that internalized what she had taught me about *being alive*, she wouldn't actually be gone. Or perhaps more accurately, I could integrate the magic of our relationship into how I lived, and in the process learn how to be more completely myself.

THE MUSIC OF HEALING

Of course, the sadness was there (oh boy was it there), and music became a big part of my healing process, of letting myself feel the grief and loss. We had a soundtrack to our relationship, a playlist she'd made full of fantastic songs that loomed large in my memory and heart. (A few of my favorites: Eagle Eye Cherry's *Save Tonight*, Pat Benetar's *We Belong*, and The Outfield's *Your Love*, which doubled as my senior solo for my acapella group.)

I had learned what it was like to truly listen to and *feel* music from her, and I wanted to claim this way of living as my own. It started by reclaiming these songs. They were full of emotion, and, drawing on what Zen had taught me, I let myself simply feel it all as I lay in bed and listened. Tears, memories, moments of elation and revelation — the playlist contained it all, and these energies washed over me again and again.

One evening towards the end of that year, I was hanging out with a few of my best friends from high school, and one of them floated an idea: *Want to go to Coachella, a music festival taking place early the next year?* I was intrigued, as I had never been to a music festival, and I sensed this trip could be part of my healing process.

I checked the lineup and saw that, outside of a few like Paul McCartney, The Killers, and Lupe Fiasco, I didn't know many of artists slated to perform. On the recommendations of some friends, I picked some acts and immersed myself in their music to prepare for the festival: Beirut, Thievery Corporation, Fleet Foxes, Girl Talk, the Yeah Yeah Yeahs, and others.

These bands became the soundtrack of my life. I put their music on before going to bed. I jammed along while working out. I burned their music onto CDs and kept them in my car. I still listened to the old playlist Clara had made now and then, but I could feel the freshness these new artists were bringing into my life. My world started to shine a little more day by day, a groove and flow that made life feel lighter.

The festival itself felt like a rebirth, pure bliss in the form of careless dancing drenched in sunlight, lots of laughter, the simplicity and sleepover vibes of our friend group camping outside together, and set after set of artists I loved. Between listening to the music in advance and the impact of more than a year of meditating, I could feel how much easier it was to pay attention, to lose myself in the music with presence and groundedness. I even met a romantic interest, and though she lived in Los Angeles, we remained friends for many years.

YES, THIS

A large part of my grappling with love and attachment resolved somewhere on that trip. I thought love was about a person and the relationship we shared. But eight months after Clara and I broke up, I felt just as "in love" at Coachella as I had been with her — I was in love with everything around me, with my life as a whole.

I realized that what we normally call love flows from a source: accepting and embracing life exactly as it is. And in this light, what my college teacher had said about love — that it's a process of letting go — started to make sense. Our lives are always changing, so loving our lives is a loving of continual changes. To do this, we have no choice but to let go of what's passed.

When DT Suzuki was sobbing at his wife's funeral, it was undoubtedly fueled by sadness, but in a larger sense, it was an expression of *yes, this*. Yes this pain, yes this grief. Tragedy is an inherent part of love, of living with an open heart. With the entirety of his being, Suzuki was fully and fearlessly embracing the heartbreak that life was offering him. That embrace was at the heart of his teaching, and is the heart of Zen as a tradition.

The breakup was my own first significant episode of *yes, this*. I felt so much aversion to the pain, but as I found ways to open up to it, I saw that it contained Aliveness. Feeling pain was, I realized, the only way I could allow Aliveness to flow.

As I returned home from the festival and reflected on the past few months, I could hardly believe how much Zen practice had transformed my life. In the past, I would get over relationships by throwing myself into dating and partying. Zen had prepared me to navigate this whole process in a way that would have been scarcely imaginable a year before.

Instead of seeking out new partners, I purposefully committed to staying single for a while as a way ensuring I didn't bypass what I was feeling. Rather than numb the pain with socializing and alcohol, I faced it. I felt it. I used the resources and emotional triggers I was naturally drawn to — music, specifically — to facilitate *embracing* what life was offering me, as painful as it was. Seeing the beauty and magic of how it all worked out, I vowed to continue to turn towards presence and let it nourish, train, and lead me going forward.

3

CHASING SHINY OBJECTS: STARTUP EDITION

GROWING up in Silicon Valley was a wild experience. My Dad worked at Sun Microsystems in the 90s. I knew the company was a big deal, but I realized just how big a deal it was when Pixar's *Toy Story* was released in November 1995. It was the first film animated entirely using computers, and it was a smashing success. At the end of the movie, the credits included a thank you to the team at Sun that built the powerful, cutting-edge computer that Pixar used to power the animation, the SparcStation2.

My Dad led that team. From that point on, when he confidently would tell me Silicon Valley was changing everything, I believed him in my bones. Even at a young age, I was aware that I was living through one of the largest and most world-changing technological and economic booms in history.

I saw how the tech industry was transforming everything around me. In the early 1990s, there were still a few working farms and a fair amount of open land in the Bay Area. Over the years, I saw these be transformed into homes and office parks. So many of my friends' parents and parents' friends were working at exciting companies, creating startups, and visibly getting wealthier. Over the 90s and 2000s, our family and so many of my friends' families moved to bigger houses, with some of them buying mansions when, as I was told, "they sold their company."

I naturally felt attracted to tech as an industry and grew up with a profound sense that *anything is possible*. In particular, entrepreneurship captured my interest — I loved the idea of creating something new in the world. When I started Athleague, I remember both the excitement and the pressure of thinking *this is my chance*.

This enthusiasm focused my mind and helped me navigate the fallout from the market crash in late summer 2008. I didn't wallow or dawdle — we needed to survive. I cut salaries to make our existing funds last longer, and because I had a great relationship with our four-person team, everyone stuck around.

We had signed up a few colleges to use our product that first year, but we were nowhere near being financially sustainable from the money they were paying us. With fundraising impossible, we had to find revenue elsewhere, and the clock was ticking.

THE RISE AND FALL

Advertising was becoming a tried and true way to make money on the internet, and our audience — casual college athletes — seemed like a logical fit for sporting goods brands. I started to pitch these companies, and lo and behold, we had strong interest from Reebok. In August 2009, after 6 months of meetings, I visited their offices outside Boston for our final pitch with their executive marketing team. A couple hours later, I was sitting in the Boston Common, a park in the center of the city, when I got the phone call: we had a deal.

Against all odds, we could keep our doors open for another couple years and, I thought, had a path to long-term viability.

I knew it was time to go all-in on making the company work, so later that month, I moved to Boston to be co-located with my team. I found an apartment in the Downtown Crossing neighborhood with one of my best friends and a couple of his friends as roommates. We quickly bonded over mind-opening conversations running late into the night on life, Zen, philosophy, startups, dating, and everything in between. My coworkers frequently came over to work and hang out at our apartment, and before we knew it, our place was the home-base for a vibrant community of friends.

Life was fun, but I didn't forget why I moved: to build Athleague into a success. And at first, things seemed to be looking alright. We were growing — by 2010, a year after I moved, we were powering the intramural sports programs for 50 colleges, reaching around 100,000 students. Just as importantly, our team had great chemistry, weathering work emergencies together, learning from our interpersonal dynamics, and growing as we discovered competencies we didn't know were there.

As time passed, though, cracks in our business began to emerge. We doubled in size from 2010 to 2011, but schools simply couldn't pay us very much, so the vast majority of our revenue was still coming from Reebok. Unfortunately, our deal with Reebok wasn't driving very many sales for them, certainly not enough to justify them paying us as much as they were. We had enough cash in the bank to last another year, but our primary pathway to financial sustainability was murky at best.

Even more troublingly, we seemed to be losing out to the other startup in our industry, IMLeagues. Even though our product was better designed and more powerful than theirs, IMLeagues was signing up two big schools for every one we landed.

It turned out that product quality wasn't quite so important for the colleges we were selling to. They were classic late adopters, skeptical about technology with a fearful, "if it ain't broke, don't fix it" mentality. IMLeagues recognized this, and with the deep pockets of a wealthy family behind them, they had a much larger customer service and sales team (whereas for us, it was just me). As a result, they were more available for impromptu phone calls and, as southerners selling to a largely heartland customer base, more familiar than we were.

Our weakness compared to IMLeagues forced me to get real about our position. I started to do the math. If the Reebok deal didn't renew, which it likely wouldn't, we needed close to a thousand schools to sign up to reach profitability, and we only had a hundred. We faced a long, uphill climb simply to be able to employ 5-10 people at market-rate salaries.

This financial reality wasn't new to me, but it took me far longer to respond to it than it should have. I'd held onto a stubborn optimism that something might shift with Reebok, but when Reebok decided to end our marketing relationship at the end of 2011, I needed to face the facts.

As the saying goes, there wasn't a *there* there. The juicy business idea that I thought we were navigating toward didn't, in fact, exist. Our growth was too slow, the market was too small, and our customers' ability to pay was too low.

In light of this, I had two options: raise new money to pivot the company or try to sell it. We explored fundraising and potential pivots, but in the end, investors weren't interested and more importantly, my heart wasn't in it. I had tried to push with all my might for 4 years, and I was exhausted.

IMLeagues was amenable to acquiring us, and though it took us many months to agree to terms, I sold the company in the summer of 2012. A little more than 5 years since its inception, I was officially done with Athleague.

PEERING BENEATH THE SURFACE

I started Athleague because I was obsessed with sports and startups growing up. It seemed like the perfect project for me. The insight that seeded Athleague was valid and even visionary (if not obvious): the internet was changing how we signed up for things. I felt that sports leagues would be managed and organized very differently in a few years (and that turned out to be true). But I didn't see the obvious — there just wasn't a great company to be built in the college intramural leagues space.

Pivoting was and is common for startups. We could have easily switched to a more impactful and profitable idea. As a team, we had even identified and dissected companies like Eventbrite, Active (which managed marathon registrations), and others that served the events market. As far back as 2009, in casual conversations, we'd speculate on how we could use our platform as a base to build a better product experience than they had.

In hindsight, *not* pivoting towards a larger market seemed so stupid. We had a great team and built a fantastic platform, yet I consistently shied away from pulling the trigger. Why?

During meditation one morning in 2011 (when I was fighting tooth and nail to make Athleague work out), I found myself mentally rehearsing a conversation about Athleague's progress with one of our investors, Ted.

"Listen, Ravi, we like the concept of Athleague and we know you've worked hard, but we can't invest more money," Ted said in our

imagined conversation. *"Even if you hit all your goals, it just won't be enough of a return for us."*

In my mind, I fought back vigorously. I explained how the market was bigger than it seemed, and how we could build additional products that would make more money. Even in these imagined conversations, part of me knew the truth, and yet I was stubbornly fighting to prove staying the course was the right decision.

I took a breath, felt my belly expand, and returned to my practice. All of a sudden, there it was: a dark pit in my stomach. My obstinance was a cover for a fear of seeming wrong, stupid, irresponsible. I was terrified of failing.

THE ELEPHANT AND THE RIDER

My fear of failure had deep roots. As I was growing up, my parents did an incredible job of encouraging me to pursue my passions. But as in so many families, there was a consistent sense that doing poorly — whether in the classroom or outside of it — was *not ok*.

I rarely had to encounter this not-okayness through my years in school. I got great grades, and from sports to debate to theater, I excelled outside the classroom. It all culminated in gaining admission to an elite program at an Ivy League school. Every significant endeavor I had dedicated myself to had basically gone well. As a result, I carried what seemed like a healthy sense of self-esteem and worthiness into adulthood.

In actuality, I never got much practice failing. What this meant was that *I needed to feel successful to know I was ok*. As a result, I chose a small idea, one that I thought would offer an easy path to startup success. As the evidence mounted that this path was not so easy after all — that neither Reebok nor colleges were likely to lead us to profitability — I couldn't really accept it and act accordingly. I had built a wall inside my head that blocked out anything that might suggest I wasn't successful.

I was scared of failure, but what this mental barrier was really blocking was an emotion: shame. I can feel the burning blood flowing through my cheeks and shoulders right now, just writing about this chapter of my life.

The simple truth of Athleague's failure was deeply embarrassing. I convinced some of the smartest investors I knew to believe in my vision and recruited a team of MIT engineers to join me on my quest. These people had trusted me with their money and livelihood, and I was, so clearly it seemed, unworthy of their confidence. To give up on intramural sports programs would be to admit my humiliating ineptitude as a startup founder. The fear of facing my unconscious shame was too big to even consider a pivot — which, ironically, would have actually *maximized* our chances of success!

But within my conscious mental logic, I thought not pivoting away from intramurals was a rational business decision. I now started to understand that *my thinking mind was functioning to get my emotional needs met* — in this case, keeping me from feeling the crippling shame of failure. If I wanted to be effective at work (and life), I needed to become more aware of how my emotional world was impacting how I was perceiving reality.

I reflected on all of this in a sign-off email to our investors (which I later edited and posted on my old Blogspot journal):

There is a last takeaway for myself as an entrepreneur that I believe, in the final analysis, will be the most important: my fear of failure and lack of self-confidence at the outset. In hindsight, 21-year-old me was approaching the entire notion of starting a company from a place of insecurity. My subconscious thinking was that the small vision of intramural leagues presented the best chance to quickly be successful.

When confronted with evidence that we should pivot into larger industries, I didn't do it because I was scared. On the outside, I projected cocky superiority toward IMLeagues; on the inside, my insecurity kept me from being honest with myself and my team.

While evaluating the effect of the subconscious on the conscious mind is nearly impossible, looking back, this is my best guess at what held us back at the most fundamental level. Thinking small and fearfully is a mistake that I'll labor to not make again.

I was understanding the power of the unconscious for the first time. In his book, *The Happiness Hypothesis*, Jonathan Haidt uses the example of a rider (the conscious, rational mind) on an elephant (the unconscious mind) for the way our minds work. The rider thinks that they're in control. In reality, not only is the elephant more powerful, but, as Haidt writes, "the rider evolved to serve the elephant, not the other way around."

And this elephant, fundamentally, wants to feel *good about itself*. I wanted to feel smart, successful — and *not* like I was failing. This simple desire drove how I framed and understood what was happening at work and across my life.

THE TRANCE OF UNWORTHINESS

These insights eventually found me because, during my years in Boston, my Zen practice continued to deepen. The honeymoon phase had ended, and I wasn't walking around in awe of the sights and sounds in my life quite so often anymore. But an unwavering faith had been lit during the unique and blissful chapter of my life in which I came into practice. I understood that Zen was working on me at a level beyond my conscious awareness — that my presence and attention were being trained *whether I felt like they were or not.*

It was at this time in my life that I started practicing with a nearby *sangha*, a community of Buddhist practitioners. Once every week or two, I'd take the Red Line subway across the Charles River, change into some gray robes, and meditate at the Cambridge Zen Center. As part of these visits, I heard *dharma* talks — lectures on Buddhist teachings — for the first time, and I got to know a few of the people there. I started sitting for up to a couple hours on Saturday mornings, and deeper experiences of quiet and insight began to find me.

I read many Buddhist books at the time, but one stood out: *Radical Acceptance* by the well-known American Buddhist teacher, Tara Brach. The book perfectly crystallized what I was starting to see inside of myself: the persistent sense that I had something to prove, that I wasn't enough on my own without external validation.

Tara calls this the "trance of unworthiness," a phrase that gave me goosebumps when I first read it and still does today. She describes it as such: "Feeling that something is wrong with us is the invisible and toxic gas we are always breathing. When we experience our lives through this lens of personal insufficiency, we are imprisoned in what I call the trance of unworthiness."

I dove headfirst into Tara's now-famous book, seeking answers to my questions about how our unconscious emotional needs affect how we live and frame our world. In the very first chapter of the book, Tara describes the "strategies [we use] to manage the pain of inadequacy" within the trance of unworthiness. My mind was blown at how easily I saw myself in each of them:

- **We hold back and play it safe rather than risking failure.** Tara writes, "We want to be instantly good at everything and avoid risky situations." This is exactly what I had done by not pivoting away from intramural leagues as our target market. I just didn't have the self-confidence to take a bigger swing.
- **We withdraw from our experience of the present moment.** "We pull away from the raw feelings of fear and shame by incessantly telling ourselves stories about what's happening in our life." I constantly told myself a story of how we were doing as a company — it was how I got by. The way I consistently avoided fear and shame is what kept us from changing directions. Had I been open to feeling them, I likely would have been able to evaluate a pivot more objectively (and intelligently).
- **We keep busy.** "Staying occupied is a socially sanctioned way of remaining distant from our pain. If we stop, we run the risk of plunging into the unbearable feeling that we are alone and utterly worthless." It would be years until I started to see the way this was rooted in the trance of unworthiness, but between work and an active social life, my life in Boston was very full.
- **We become our own worst critics.** "The running commentary in our mind reminds us over and over that we always screw up." I didn't realize this was going on until I read these words! My inner critic had been operating underneath my awareness, chipping away at my confidence in myself and our team.
- **We focus on other people's faults.** "The more inadequate we feel, the more uncomfortable it is to admit our faults. Blaming others temporarily relieves us from the weight of failure." IMLeague's product

sucked. Our customers were stupid. Looking back, I noticed how often I was mentally punching down on others as a form of trying to feel good about myself.

I had never realized how such seemingly different behaviors had a single root. So often, my basic orientation to myself was that of not good enough — which naturally led to looking outside to feel a sense of worthiness.

This was a life-changing realization. Starting Athleague was, in large part, a result of "looking outside to feel a sense of worthiness." Making it successful would be proof of my intelligence, ingenuity, and value as a human being.

My desire to build Athleague was directly proportional to my believing that this would happen. As it became more and more clear that Athleague would fail, my energy to work on it slowly slipped away.

But there was a silver lining to this process: it started to open up space for me to discover what truly mattered to me.

4

RUNNING INTO REAL PASSION

"This is not the end!"

I was speaking to a crowd of almost 5,000 people. Without fail, the closest thousand or so replied back, "This is not the end!" so that the people in the back could hear. This was the "People's Mic" in action, a way to amplify voices since sound amplification (i.e. a regular mic and speakers) was not allowed in public spaces.

It was early December 2011, and we were hours away from the police raiding Occupy Boston to shut down the encampment that we had so lovingly created over the past 3 months. Over the next 10 minutes, I shared my experiences within our movement's various working groups and encouraged people to stay connected and involved as our physical home was being destroyed.

After every sentence, I would pause, waiting for my words to be repeated so all could hear. It was a funny style of speaking, but it always left me feeling both powerful and oddly relaxed, having a moment to stop, listen to my words, and breathe instead of moving from one thought to the next.

I had rarely spoken publicly before – and never to a crowd of this size – but over these few months, it ended up happening quite often. In this critical moment of transition for our movement, I felt compelled to say something, given how deep a part of my life the Occupy movement had become.

This journey began three months earlier. As I was walking home from a friend's place one evening in September 2011, I noticed a crowd of people gathered in the Boston Common at almost the exact same spot where I received that call from Reebok two years earlier. I walked over to inquire what was going on, and they told me they were planning an "occupation."

Occupy Wall Street had started days prior in New York City and was gaining immense traction, as tens of thousands of people flooded downtown Manhattan in protest of wealth inequality, unjust economic policies, and corporate greed. The burgeoning movement seemed to be pointing out core economic and political truths with clarity and resolve, and I wanted to learn more. I talked with the Occupy Boston organizers for a little while and decided to hang around.

Two nights later, I found myself helping set up the Occupy Boston encampment in Dewey Square across from South Station, putting up a few tents, a welcome desk, and other infrastructure. I went back the next day to keep assisting and again the day after that. Before I knew it, it became an everyday thing.

UNDERSTANDING THE MOVEMENT

The contrast between the energy I felt joining Occupy Boston made my waning enthusiasm for Athleague all the more clear. The movement catalyzed in me a deeper sense of passion than I had ever known. First and foremost, I learned so much. I had known about wealth inequality, but the simple framing of it being a movement for the "99%" of people was direct and powerful. It started out as a critique of the big banks and the bailouts they received in the aftermath of the 2008 financial crash. From there, it quickly grew to more broadly articulate how the wealthiest 1% of people and corporations had (and have) captured and corrupted the government. At the core, we were protesting *how we think about the economy* in the first place.

This analysis resonated with me. While attending the Wharton School of Business as an undergraduate, I saw how the curriculum at a supposedly prestigious school blatantly ignored aspects of capitalism and how its policies affect real people and communities. I distinctly remember sitting in class as a renowned economics professor tried to tell us that rent control was harmful for society because it kept the housing market from reaching equilibrium. It was almost comical – at no point did he mention gentrification, the social cost to communities, or the broader impact on society when tenants in whole areas of cities are no longer able to afford rent.

The economic dogma they taught felt like a religion. There was rarely any curiosity about where wealth disparities came from or any willingness to explore the effect concentrated wealth has on society.

Later, I would come to understand how deep the school's ties were to the financial elite. Graduates would go on to work at hedge funds and big banks – the higher the GPA, the more prestigious the firm. These companies would turn around and donate large sums of money to the school. Without any explicit rules dictating it, the content of our education came second to making sure this *quid pro quo* was flowing freely. So actually, my school was teaching us how economic and political systems worked after all – just not in the classroom, but rather by example.

Many of my friends from college had gone on to work for these financial firms and made boatloads of money. It never made any sense to me: they weren't *creating* anything, be it food or goods or equipment or even websites. They were just using money to make more money. Some of their hedge funds would employ tactics like "high-frequency trading" (HFT) – fast computers and high-speed internet connections, basically – to make trades more quickly than others. They would literally see which way the market was moving and use their technological advantages to profit. It was the perfect metaphor for the vast majority of the financial sector: reverse Robin Hood, different forms of the wealthy stealing from everyone who didn't have the same access and privileges.

None of this was a secret. A viral Matt Taibbi article in *Rolling Stone* popularized the image of the most well-known bank, Goldman Sachs, as a "vampire squid" sucking on society. Books and movies (most notably *The Big Short*) made it painfully clear how the banks' greed and illegal activity vastly exacerbated the 2008 crash. Yet in the end, no one went to jail, and the American people ended up having to bail the banks out, even while so many regular people lost their homes and jobs.

BROADENING MY PERSPECTIVE

A sense of justice and service had awakened inside of me. I threw myself into helping the movement with all my spare hours, usually 6-11pm most days. I joined the Tech and Community Outreach working groups, and before I knew it, I was venturing across the city, building ties with various nonprofits and activist groups and organizing joint actions and marches.

Of all of these trips taken and relationships built, I spent the most time at town halls affiliated with the Occupy the Hood movement (an offshoot of Occupy Wall Street) in Roxbury, a historically Black neighborhood located southwest of Boston. These were facilitated by a charismatic community organizer, Darrin Howell, and they helped me understand how deeply the system was stacked against underprivileged neighborhoods and communities of color.

The list of challenges there seemed endless. Since schools are funded from property taxes, the education system was chronically underpaying teachers, underfunded, and, as a result, underperforming. Everything from hospitals and grocery stores required a trip outside the neighborhood because building these crucial parts of infrastructure was rarely profitable in inner city neighborhoods. Given poor public transportation and people needing to work multiple jobs, the simple act of getting medical care or healthy food faced not just deep financial hurdles but logistical ones as well. Redlining and other forms of housing discrimination made it difficult to build wealth and own property for average members of the community.

And we haven't even mentioned the vastness of systemic racism and police brutality that they and so many other communities experience every day.

In the years to come, racial justice (and the inner process of how we internalize racial identity) would become a big part of my work and life. It was on these visits to Roxbury that I began to encounter the realities of race in America outside of the rap songs I grew up with.

REALIZING ALIVENESS

I could feel myself palpably *on fire* every day, fueled by a sense of justice, service, and connection with the amazing people around me. The movement unlocked empathy, energy, and an entire systemic perspective that I had never known before. The passionate energy I felt reminded me of the early days of Athleague but more true, more *alive*.

I remember the peaceful anticipation and relaxed excitement of the five-minute walk from my apartment to the Occupy Boston location in Dewey Square. Even though I was extremely busy organizing and protesting, I felt more present, compassionate, and awake than I ever had. I met people from profoundly different walks of life – from MIT PhD students to folks struggling with homelessness – and felt my heart open over and over with each of them.

It was Aliveness, the natural consequence of being engaged in something that spoke to and flowed from my Inner World. The energy it gave me was natural, renewable, and opened up access to the best parts of myself. By contrast, I noticed how much of my energy for Athleague was linked to getting something out of it, achieving an outcome. With Occupy Boston, it was energizing simply to *be* there and contribute in whatever ways I could. In a deeper way than ever before, I was touching a life rooted in what was true for me and learning how it felt to do things for their own sake rather than to gain something – and I was feeling the power that came from living like this.

5

THE MIRROR OF BURNING MAN

DURING THE OCCUPY MOVEMENT, I met a bunch of people who had been to an arts festival I'd heard a little bit about: Burning Man. This wasn't a coincidence. Occupy and Burning Man both shared a core organizing principle: empowering people to contribute in whatever way they were called to. At Occupy, this meant joining or starting whichever working groups or projects that one felt would best serve the movement.

Burning Man takes a similar approach. It's a festival in the harsh northern Nevada desert in which participants provide the art (rather than festivals like Coachella, where all the entertainment is organized by a company for profit). I had seen some amazing pictures of the sculptures artists would build, and I'd wanted to go for a few years. After selling Athleague, I was finally free from the usual back-to-school season workload and made plans to attend in the late summer of 2012 with a few friends.

As we drove up to the gates, the desert stretched out in front of us, with mountains in the distance glowing pink in the fading sun. When we presented our tickets, the greeters asked if it was our first time. We nodded, and they instructed us to get out of the car and roll around the dusty, barren ground (the standard initiatory ritual for "virgins," or first-timers).

We had arrived. I flipped through the guidebook, stunned at the array of events that various camps were putting on. On my first full day, I set off to explore. I started with an hour of breathwork, attended a lecture on local desert ecology, eye-gazed and played "authentic relating games" with strangers, and went to a panel entitled "BDSM 101", which offered eye-opening perspectives on kink and its potential to open us up to play, pleasure, and love. Up next was sunset yoga, but as I was biking over (biking is the primary mode of transporta-tion), I noticed the wind pick up. Within a few minutes, the desert sands were all around me – I couldn't see a thing. I waited, but the dust storm kept going. *Bummer, I'm going to miss yoga,* I thought.

Then the irony hit me, and I laughed. I was dejected to be missing a practice about embodiment and presence, somehow completely ignoring the fact that the dust storm was offering me these in a more immersive way than any yoga class ever could.

Goggles and dust mask on, I stopped and looked around. The dust had gotten so thick that I could hardly see my own hands. It was enthralling, and it just kept going. Half an hour later (I think?), the dust finally cleared. My senses once again exploded. In the blink of an eye, there was music all around me, art pieces stretching high into the sky and deep into the horizon, and bikes, people, and color everywhere.

One of Burning Man's ten principles is immediacy – being in the moment and *experiencing* what's happening right now. Caught in the dust storm, this principle hit me like a ton of bricks. The next day, I tossed the festival guidebook aside and set out intent on having no plan. Every time I noticed my curiosity perk up, I stopped and explored. I spent an hour walking slowly around a 20-foot tall, fire-breathing metal dragon, soaking in its beauty and marveling at its engineering from every angle. It felt like one of my first meditation sessions during my senior year of college, when I just sat and stared at a piece of lint on the floor. I was lost in awe.

Unlike the day before, I felt no fomo (fear of missing out) when I heard my friends' stories back at camp that evening. I had spent the day doing exactly what mattered to me, when it mattered to me. I thought my first day, with its planning and activity, was full of Aliveness. And yet this second day, with nothing planned, had brought me to life in a much deeper, more fundamental way.

It was a different way of living. In my regular life, I'd try to optimize my travel to get to where I'm going as quickly and efficiently as I could. At Burning Man, I purposefully only gave myself a loose sense of where I was going and welcomed getting lost and seeing what happened.

NAVIGATING ANEW

I was, in essence, deemphasizing my normal ways of navigating life and, instead, letting my sense of wonder and curiosity lead. To this day, this is the primary practice for me at Burning Man. Each year that I attend, it offers a present, dynamic, living-and-breathing encounter with what's alive.

This radical following-of-my-Aliveness has produced countless moments of transformation. One of the most lasting things from that first Burn was that I discovered dance for what felt like the first time. Before I went, dancing was something that felt awkward and forced, and I was pretty "meh" when it came to electronic music.

But one evening, after a peaceful sunset meditation session, I was out with friends, and we stumbled onto a music set that was instantly transporting. The wacky, dubstep bass intermingled with a beautiful trombone riff and knocked something loose inside of me. It hit all of us simultaneously, and our whole group got off our bikes and started dancing, *hard*. I didn't even feel like *I* was dancing, but rather that the music was dancing me.

Whatever magic was unlocked that night more than a decade ago has not faded – dancing has become one of the greatest joys of my life. The dynamic of "the music dancing me" has been helpful in understanding a fundamental tenet of Aliveness: letting go and letting the energy of the moment move me (literally or metaphorically) as a form of expression and presence.

Through all of these experiences, I was learning something about how I wanted to live: presence, embodiment, and flow. All week, I kept returning to my body and exploring what I was feeling, what was alive for me. From the endless art to dance to spending time at the Temple (a sacred space for grief, healing, and gratitude), the diversity of the offerings allowed me to connect with the full range of my humanity and emotions.

LIFE AS A GIFT

Despite everything – the art, dancing, workshops, lectures, and everything else – I believe there's one core reason why people so consistently experience Burning Man as transformational: *kindness*.

Each experience at the festival is crafted and constructed by a fellow attendee and then offered freely, known as gift culture. This was, to say the least, mind-boggling. For every music set encountered, there were a group of people who hauled the equipment and set up the sound system. For every 20-foot fire-breathing dragon, there was a team of artists that spent the summer designing it and then got to the desert a week early to build the piece. For every cup of coffee or meal shared, someone bought the food and then cooked and lovingly served it.

But the gifts and offerings weren't just material. One of my most vivid memories is how quick people were to help. As we were setting up our camp, one of my campmates was carrying a heavy box of tools, clearly struggling to hold it up. Before I could take a single step in their direction, someone had stopped their bike, hopped off, and grabbed the one end of the box. This person was a total stranger, and yet they didn't think twice before jumping in to be of assistance.

This sort of thing happened all the time. When I first experienced this aspect of Burning Man, I was aghast. I was so convinced of our usual way of understanding how things worked and our relationship with each other that this new world didn't compute. I would double-check when I got a drink at a bar: "I don't have to pay for this?"

Often during my first time out there, I'd look across the open desert filled with art and wonder about the thousands of artists who dedicated their own time and money to build something beautiful to share. But by the end of the week, it made sense – I could feel in the people around me the genuine sense of pleasure that was driving the spirit of gifting. There was a spark of generosity and kindness on a scale that, until then, I hadn't thought possible.

What a stark dichotomy from the rest of my life. These days, Burning Man gets a lot of grief for turning into a rich, tech bro faux-utopia, and there is definitely some truth to this critique. But I believe what makes it so valuable is the contrast it draws to the rest of our lives and the possibility it offers of an entirely different way of relating with each other. At its core is the truth that our lives are a gift to enjoy and share.

In less than a year, Occupy Boston and Burning Man had left me feeling more alive than ever. I was starting to sense my well of passion ran much deeper than I ever knew, and that its expression could take more vast forms than I thought possible.

6

THE DEFAULT WORLD

COMING HOME from that first Burning Man was hard. I felt tight, un-curious, and selfish mind-states seep back as I readjusted to my regular life, and the vague sense of gloom and sadness that accompanied these. This was so common it had a name – post-playa depression ("playa" is the name for the desert where the event takes place). It wasn't that I was merely bored or lacked stimulation, but rather that the emotional and interpersonal depth and expansiveness of that week in the desert stood in such stark contrast with the rest of my life.

The saving grace within this was how apparently normal my reaction was. Experienced Burners told me my ennui was simply a consequence of coming back to what they called the "default world."

I still remember the immediate sense of "aha!" that hit me when I first heard those words. The way I had lived thus far was my *default* life. It made complete sense that the reason this happened was because the default *world* I was simply responding to the conditions, incentives, and value systems that were considered normal and all around me.

There are two layers to the default world: first, at a literal level, it is the world – with its customs, economy, technology, political structure, etc. – that we are defaulted into simply by being born.

Second and more deeply, unless we intentionally disrupt the process, it exerts a pull that *defaults us into its priorities* and causes us to lose sight of our own. Many parts of our culture and society have a vested interest in our unworthiness and our validation-seeking. These are fuel for the economic and cultural engines that society seems to run on.

The default world is the chief villain in this book. It refers to the set of external conditions, ideologies, and material realities that exist all around us. Over time, these take root in our Inner World as limiting mindsets and beliefs as to who we are, what's important, and what we're capable of.

Specifically, the default world wants to harvest our energy and uniqueness for profit in one way or another. Instagram *wants* us to post frequently (that's how they make money). Clothing companies want us to buy their latest fashions, the ones that make us feel temporarily desirable or special. Food companies aren't interested in our health – they want us to stuff our faces with junk food. Our physical, emotional, and spiritual health pale in importance to these entities' profit.

The default world is the vast momentum of society and the beliefs that hold it together. It consists of the political, economic, and social systems we live within. It includes our cultural myths, media, entertainment, and advertising. It is the background circumstances and conditions that make modern life what it is.

In the default world, some choices, ideas, and ways of living seem normal, and alternatives to it are countercultural and weird. The impact of the default world on our lives is endless

– as I turned this lens on parts of my life, I started to see the ways it had affected me and the choices I made.

DEFAULT DATING

In 2010, I was navigating my first winter in Boston (shocker: it was cold) when I randomly met someone special, Joy, while out at an Indian dance show on Valentine's Day. We had instant chemistry and started dating that summer when she moved to nearby Cambridge.

Joy seemed absolutely perfect. She was smart, a fact underscored by her attending the Law *and* Business graduate schools at Harvard. She turned heads in every room she walked into, and I was more attracted to her than perhaps anyone I had ever met. To top it off, she was Indian and spoke Hindi, which I knew my parents would love.

And for some reason, she was into me, so sure about wanting to date me that it was a bit overwhelming. That someone like her would want to be with me was a form of approval I had never quite received.

This validation was magnified by everyone around me. One time, we were visiting New York and grabbing dinner with one of my best friends. Joy had to leave early, and after she did, my friend turned to me and confidently said, "Wow, you're definitely marrying her." At that moment, I remember so clearly thinking *well, yeah, I guess I am*.

I don't quite know where the metaphor of "checking boxes" came from, but I found myself using it when describing her. She, very clearly, checked all the boxes, and the people in my life tended to quickly reflect this back to me when they met her.

When we were present with each other, our relationship was pretty fantastic. We laughed a lot together, bonded over our shared heritage, and had a repertoire that was both silly and relaxed as well as heady and intellectual. During my ups and downs of being an entrepreneur, she was usually supportive, offering a listening ear, a fun date when I needed it – and even astute startup advice.

I remember being surprised one night when she had a piercing analysis of a particular product strategy we were exploring for Athleague – and then being surprised that I was surprised! I had made her intelligence an object, neatly visible in the form of her Harvard JD/MBA. In doing so, I obscured my ability to simply *appreciate and enjoy* her beautiful mind and what it brought into my life. In some crevice of my thinking, I had gotten it backwards, dating her because of the marker or status that various aspects of her identity represented rather than being in everyday contact with who she actually was.

THE DIRTY ENERGY OF VALIDATION

The complicated thing about all of this is that "getting it backward" *gave me energy*. When I went to events with her at Harvard, *I felt smart*. When I saw how others reacted to me when they found out I was dating her, *I felt important*. The whole thing was intoxicating. I just *felt good* with her.

Like any relationship, this one was a reflection of what was going on in my life at the time. When I met Clara three years prior, I was a Senior in college and freshly funded entrepreneur; Clara's expansiveness and enthusiasm mirrored my own. By 2010, I was stretched thin, trying to navigate a startup through an economic recession, and already flirting with professional failure. The affirmation I received from Joy and the people in my life when they met her captured me completely because I wasn't getting that sort of positivity from the place I was investing the vast majority of my life energy (Athleague).

While I didn't have the words for it back then, I was hooked into a cycle of external validation. I've come to understand this as a sort of dirty energy, a bit like fossil fuels. In one sense, it truly works – it gets us from point A to B. When relationship doubts arose within me, other people's reassurances or the tangible markers of her qualities gave me a clear reason to keep dating her. They served as a constant reminder of how wonderful Joy was.

But, deep down, I knew what I was feeling wasn't actually about her. In my own unworthiness, I had turned Joy into an object for my sense of self-esteem. It would be years before I had any awareness of patriarchy and how its conditioning was part of this objectification, but even in the moment, I could feel something wasn't right.

As our relationship progressed over the next few years, the validation I got from dating her began to blind me to the living, breathing human in front of my face. The more that my relationship satisfaction came from the *story* of being with her, the less I was present to the *experience* of it. This was a slow death sentence for us as a couple: the stories we tell ourselves are not a source of life.

She came to represent the default world validation that I both craved and knew, deep down, wasn't real love (nor what I actually wanted). What makes me sad, in hindsight, is that *she was grappling with the exact same thing.* Hardly anyone goes to a place like Harvard without craving social approval. She was caught in her own battle between the life others expect of her and living her truth.

In a different world with older and wiser versions of us, we may have been able to make our struggle a shared one, something that brought us closer together. Instead, I played the role of dream-chasing founder, and she that of play-it-safe careerist. I was irresponsible and not there for her; she was boring and stayed within her comfort zone.

Eventually, these dynamics grew heavy, and I ended it. Looking back, I wasn't breaking up with her, but with what she represented in my mind: conditioning around what my life should be about, status symbols, and an obsession with what other people thought. It was sad but also a personal victory, a moment of choosing a true life.

Overall, it was still a beautiful relationship with many wonderful moments and lasting lessons. We were deeply attracted to each other and tried our best to make it work, so I don't have regrets. And in case you're wondering, Joy figured out how to throw off the chains of the default world: In the decade since we broke up, she quit her corporate law job and moved to India to be an actress and model, danced in music videos across the globe, and wrote a book, *The Freelance Mindset*, encapsulating her wisdom navigating the creative life and professional world. We're still good friends, and it's been a joy (pun intended) to see her wandering, passionate career take shape.

MEANING-MAKING FOR PROFIT

As I saw how my mind was grabbing onto external markers as vehicles for validation, I began to recognize status symbol dynamics all around me.

Around this time, one of my good friends was getting engaged. He had wanted to get a diamond ring, but his partner said she preferred a sapphire one. They got into an argument, and it wasn't until he began to learn about the history of diamond rings that he began to shift his perspective. As he shared his learnings, I realized diamond rings were the perfect example of how status markers are created and the impact they have on how we experience reality.

The idea of getting engaged specifically with a diamond ring is the result of a marketing campaign from the 1940s. Amidst falling diamond prices, the De Beers Diamond Company hired the advertising agency N.W. Ayer to promote diamonds in the United States. A 2015 article in *The Atlantic* outlines the strategy that they came up with for popularizing the concept:

"The folks at Ayer set out to persuade young men that diamonds (and only diamonds) were synonymous with romance, and that the measure of a man's love (and even his personal and professional success) was directly proportional to the size and quality of the diamond he purchased. Young women, in turn, had to be convinced that courtship concluded, invariably, in a diamond.

Ayer inserted these messages into the nooks and crannies of popular culture. Movie stars were given diamonds to use as symbols of indestructible love. In addition, the agency offered stories and photographs to magazines and newspapers that would stress the size of diamonds that celebrities presented to their loved ones. They also gave lecturers [promoting] the diamond engagement ring to thousands of girls in assemblies and classrooms in leading educational institutions around the country."

Before the marketing campaign, less than 10% of engagement rings had a diamond. Within a few decades, that number jumped to over 80%. Diamonds became the unquestioned standard for getting engaged, and demand for them soared.

Companies like De Beers made record profits, and we, the people, got another thing to buy, a costly custom that we now enforce with each other. We collectively commoditized a profound expression of love in a way that often triggers a sense of inadequacy and disappointment for all but the very rich. The damage didn't stop there: largely out of Western sight, the diamond mining industry was a disaster for Africa, with local warlords seizing mines and using the profits to fund violence. Despite this, Western companies continued to turn a blind eye to their role in the conflict.

None of us had any choice about diamond rings. We were born into a world that assumes them by default, and to step outside this custom opens one up to ridicule and judgment.

What's most malicious about diamond rings is that they cause us to lose our bearing as to what real love is and where it exists. (Hint: it's not outside of us.) For so many reasons – to fit in, to feel tangibly wanted, to have an ambiguity-free way of measuring love – we take this external status symbol and plant it inside of us. The marker of a ring replaces the fullness of perhaps the most powerful emotion we can feel, shrinking our whole life.

I started to see how, in many ways, this diamond ring scheme was not so different from my relationship with Joy. I was so caught up in what she represented that I actually forgot what this was all supposed to be about: love. In the process, I was diminishing my inner trust and handcuffing my self-worth even more thoroughly to external validation.

DIAMOND RINGS, EVERYWHERE

From cars and clothes to social media and beyond, there are diamond rings all around us. These rings fill our lives with scoreboards. Trapped in the trance of unworthiness, trying to measure up to the standards of the default world can grow to be our entire life framework.

That I could (and did and at times still do!) live my life based on these scoreboards is terrifying. Love is *not* where a partner went to school or how other people react to them or the size of a diamond – love is how we show up every day with the people who matter most. We're never going to be satisfied with the number of Instagram followers we have because what we're really seeking is connection, intimacy, and being deeply understood by others. We won't feel rich with all the money in the world if we don't understand what we actually value as *wealth*. To try to get our deep, human needs met in quantified, impersonal ways is only going to stress us out and leave us unsatisfied, like trying to quench our thirst with pictures of water.

Money, power, fame, status, efficiency – they all elevate some attribute that we mistake as well-being. In chasing them, we forget what it actually means to *be well*: that what we're really after is wealth, safety, community, acceptance, and ease.

There's nothing wrong with this whole "diamond ring symbolizing love" thing as a consensual game of make-believe. We can see our conditioning and choose it – if it were meaningful to a partner and financially doable, I would buy one. What's important, though, is that we see the confusion of marker with reality. It's one of the principal ways the default world hooks us into its logic and disconnects us from our true lives.

7

THE WATER WE SWIM IN

THE BRIGHT RAYS of the morning sun blinded my eyes as I emerged from the subway station at Broadway-Lafayette in the chic SoHo neighborhood of Manhattan. As my vision adjusted, I noticed two figures towering over me.

They were easily 20 feet tall, dressed only in their underwear. The man was meticulously muscled, the woman had shapely curves, and their white yet ever-so-slightly tanned skin reflected the beaming morning light. Despite their nearly naked bodies, the billboard they were on made it clear they were part of an effort to sell clothing.

It was late 2012, and I was on a trip to New York to attend a talk by the Dalai Lama. I had been meditating on the subway ride, and as a result, I felt and heard my inner reaction quite clearly. My body tensed up, and I distinctly remember thinking: "Wow, I'm never going to be that." White, impossibly in shape (literally, as they were probably photo edited to look that way), a paragon of modern beauty standards — they represented qualities that felt clearly out of reach.

This moment might seem benign or unimportant. We encounter billboards like this all the time. Yet, that simple moment of awareness as I gazed up at their bodies helped crystallize all I had been learning about the default world and how ubiquitous it is in our experience of life.

The purpose of this ad was to sell a product, but its method for doing so, like most ads, was to stir up my insecurity. My not feeling good enough was the exact trigger the company was using to get me to buy their underwear.

The message of the insecurity encouraged by this ad was straightforward: *those bodies are better than my body*. The entire logic of the billboard rested on this being true. I might not be interested in clothes, but simply by walking off the subway and looking up, I received the suggestion of this value system.

Most ads rest upon a similar status hierarchy. Certain kinds of bodies, clothing, and brands are appropriate for being literally lifted up and put on a pedestal, while others are not. This clothing ad is just one tiny thread in a thick rope of messages we get about sexiness and belonging that centers not just these bodies but a whole way of being: what one needs to wear, look like, and even act like in order to be desirable.

We don't ask for these billboards to show up. They're thrown in our paths by default, and we have to deal with the impact they have on our Inner World.

We may think this sort of default world conditioning doesn't affect us anymore. Almost 20 years into the practice of peering ever more closely into my mind and how it works, I have concluded that I will never know the depths of how influenceable I am. I know there is a part of me still yearning for acceptance and worthiness, willing to buy into default world beliefs to try to fulfill those needs even when I'm consciously rejecting them.

DEFAULT WATER

David Foster Wallace begins his 2005 graduation speech at Kenyon College with this short parable:

There are these two young fish swimming along, and they happen to meet an older fish swimming the other way, who nods at them and says, "Morning, boys. How's the water?" The two young fish swim on for a bit, and then eventually, one of them looks over at the other and goes, "What the hell is water?"

This is a simple story with an important truth. The most obvious, realities are often the ones that are hardest to see and talk about. Stated as an English sentence, of course, this is just a banal plati- tude, but the fact is that in the day-to-day trenches of adult exis- tence, banal platitudes can have a life or death importance, or so I wish to suggest to you this dry and lovely morning.

I regularly re-listen to this talk for the inspiration and clarity Wallace offers. One of his main points is that the water we're all swimming in is, essentially, the default world.

In this water, our body, our intelligence, our clothes, our rela- tionships, our money, our jobs and hobbies, even our friends and communities – none of it is good enough without external validation. Whether on purpose or merely as cultural momentum, the default world is telling us we can't just be ourselves.

This is what we're up against. The default world buries itself inside of our skin, camouflaging as things we think we want. It shapes what we value, how we live, and, at the most funda- mental level, who we think we are. It starts off as someone else's ideas, but these beliefs eventually become our own. We perpetuate the values of the default world with the people in our lives and within ourselves.

SETTING A NEW COURSE

Even back then, I knew that above all else, I wanted a true life. While I didn't use the word "vow" until a year later, I began to understand my journey of Aliveness as needing a sustained commitment. Until I took a stand, I would continue to be blown about by the winds of the default world. I perceived the mountain that was separating me from living my truth, and I was prepared to do what must be done to climb it.

But I didn't quite know what that "what" was. Occupy Boston and Burning Man had shown me that when I got outside of the default world, I could readily and more profoundly connect with what brought me to life, with my Inner World. I wanted to explore this connection, to stabilize it so I could use it to guide my life. Whatever I did next, I didn't want to wake up halfway through and lose interest. I had to learn (and wanted to experience) what made my heart sing.

I decided this was mandatory for me, an inner education clearly worth investing in. With the small amount of money I had from the Athleague acquisition, I began to plot my escape from the default Western world: spending 2013 backpacking wherever my heart took me. It would prove to be the most pivotal chapter of my life yet.

PART II

YES TO THE MESS AND MAGIC

You know, nothing can stop me but loss of breath, and I'm still breathing, so it's still on.
Tupac Shakur

You do not have to be good.
You do not have to walk on your knees
for a hundred miles through the desert, repenting.
You only have to let the soft animal of your body
love what it loves.
Mary Oliver

Let yourself be silently drawn by the strange pull of what you truly love.
Rumi

8

SCREAMING YES

I TUNED into the appropriate channel on my handheld radio and waited. The snow-capped peaks of the Himalayas poked out behind the stage, and even though the morning was warm, their tops were covered in snow. It was June 2013, and I was attending a teaching that the Dalai Lama was offering at his home monastery in Dharamsala, India on the first three chapters of Shantideva's *Guide to the Bodhisattva's Way of Life*, one of my favorite books. Because the teachings were given in His Holiness's native tongue, Tibetan, I was listening to the live translation via short-distance radio.

Eventually, the Dalai Lama began speaking, and the translator's voice came through my headphones: "Today is the fourth and final day of this teaching. We will finish the third chapter this morning, and in the afternoon, I will preside over an empowerment ceremony where anyone who so wishes will have the opportunity to take the Bodhisattva Vow. I will begin by explaining what the Vow is and what it entails, and I ask you to consider if you feel called to take this Vow today."

I sat up straighter. I didn't remember this being on the schedule. I had only read about the Bodhisattva Vow and its prominence in Buddhist training. All of a sudden, the opportunity to take it *with the Dalai Lama himself* was right in front of me. I felt my insides scream *YES* before I really knew what was going on.

That afternoon, the Dalai Lama asked those who wished to take the Vow to come to the front of the room. Of the thousands of people attending the teachings, a few hundred of us moved to the front of the space and knelt. The Dalai Lama recited the Vows and we repeated after him:

- *Sentient beings are numberless — I vow to benefit them.*
- *Desires are inexhaustible — I vow to put an end to them.*
- *The teachings are boundless — I vow to master them.*
- *The Buddha way is unattainable — I vow to attain it.*

I let the words wash over me, repeating each line after the Dalai Lama spoke them. Even in this first encounter, I felt the impossibility contained in each sentence. Putting an end to desires? Mastering boundless teachings? Attaining an unattainable way?

Not quite knowing what it meant or what I had done, I felt myself stepping into a new era, moving through what my teacher calls a "life pivot point." As I prepared to leave for my first silent meditation retreat in Ladakh the next morning, I could feel the energy that the Vows were already bringing me.

THE VOW OF ALIVENESS

In the ensuing years, I would encounter versions of this Vow in the various Buddhist centers where I practiced. When I finally found Zen Mountain Monastery, I would chant these

Vows every evening. Across all Buddhist traditions, vows are regularly made and re-made. Through years of repetition, I've felt their power seep into my bones.

These vows are not a rote formality. They are a life preserver within the overwhelming waves of the default world – or as I've come to understand them, an *Aliveness* preserver. They're a response to the simple reality that, at all moments, the default world stands ready to devour us. To contend with its fog and confusion takes a profound commitment, one that I renew every day.

Understanding this *technique* of vows – how they sculpt, protect, and focus our minds and hearts – inspired me to dig deeper, to articulate a vow that's personal, specific to my (ever-evolving) experience.

My Vow of Aliveness is simple: to prioritize what brings me to life over what numbs me, to choose presence over distraction, to trust my inner truth over external validation. It's a pledge to give my energy to the spark of life within me rather than my habits of avoidance and inertia. It's a faith that the specific circumstances of my life, flawed as they may seem, are the exact entry point I need to bring my truest, deepest self into being. This Vow is a compass, shelter, and ultimately, a path.

Every day, I'm confronted with my tendencies to avoid parts of myself and my life, to just keep floating in the direction in which the default world is nudging me.

My Vow is to go in a different direction, to trust and follow the Aliveness I feel inside of me. What comes out of this Vow is more peace and energy and less chaos and confusion. It's a power that cuts through the default world and keeps me connected to the feeling of life flowing through my veins. "Vow" as part of the title of this book came to me relatively late in the writing process, but once it did, it gripped me. The stories of my life are the stories of my Vow.

INTRODUCING THE INNER WORLD

Functionally, the Vow has a straightforward purpose: nurturing my connection with my Inner World. Occupy Boston and Burning Man had started to show me what my life might feel like if I let go of the reins a bit and allowed my Inner World to guide me.

If the default world is the enemy in our story, the Inner World is the hero. It's the source of the mess and magic that we're saying yes to, and it will take center stage from here on out. It is the wild, unseen inner landscape that comprises the core of who we are inside. It's our most profound truths: our hopes, dreams, fears, creative instincts, likes/dislikes, inner-most thoughts, the various aspects of our personality, and so much more.

For example, during the backpacking trip I'll tell you all about in the next chapter, I found myself wandering through ancient ruins overwhelmed with awe and wonder. These ruins were touching something profound within me, a spark that came directly from my Inner World. I had never known how deeply I was moved by Indian and Middle Eastern culture and history. As I traveled there and immersed myself in these places and their traditions, something came alive inside of me.

Other people may feel a similar connection, but no two sparks are alike. No one else experiences the exact same thing that I did. The unique conditions that produce this reaction inside of me are *the terrain of my Inner World*. Similarly, there's stuff that uniquely triggers your sense of passion and wonder – the source of that passion and wonder is *your*

Inner World. In the default world, we're all chasing the same things and end up in antagonistic competition. Our Inner Worlds, in contrast, guide us towards that which is uniquely ours.

The Inner World *includes* our conditioning – it is no accident that I'm Indian and have an interest in Indian history. And yet, it simultaneously *transcends* the specifics of our lives, plunging us deep into the freshness and flow of being our true selves and feeling completely *alive*. When we are connected with our Inner World, our relationship to conditioning changes. The helpful pieces of it guide us into passion and purpose, while the unhelpful parts rise to the surface and wash away as we grow more aware of what's going on inside of us.

Just like meditation practice does not involve consciously wrestling with our thoughts, connecting with our Inner World isn't dependent on intellectually understanding what's going on. The point is not the reasons for wonder but simply to notice it, to *feel* it, to begin to trust that we're encountering something meaningful, even sacred.

The experiences of Occupy Boston, Burning Man, and this upcoming backpacking trip taught me how I wanted to live – how I could say *yes, this* at the level of my whole life. And the Inner World is my way of understanding *what* I was saying "yes, this" to.

When I returned to the default world of my life in America, I applied these lessons to my life. My Inner World had become my north star, my means of navigating work, dating, Zen practice, and life as a whole. The struggles were plenty – as you'll see – but the power and clarity of staying in touch with my Aliveness gave me a lens that brought clarity, simplicity, and focus to my days.

9

HOW TO LEAVE AND NEVER
COME BACK

AT THE END OF 2012, I knew I wanted to get out, to travel the world and explore what brought me to life. The question then became where I wanted to "get out" *to*. Zen practice had become the most important part of my life, and I knew I wanted to prioritize Buddhism, meditation, and self-discovery. With this lens, the primary destination of the trip became obvious: India.

I had been to my homeland many times, but each time was the same two-week trip to see family (including 36 hours of travel time each way and usually two or three days of being sick with a stomach flu). But even in the glimpses I got during these short visits, I could feel the spirituality of the country pulsing, informing and guiding the ways people lived and interacted. I wanted to explore this aspect of the culture and knew part of the trip would involve living and practicing in a Buddhist monastery.

My experience with Occupy Boston provided the second lens for the trip: activism and community. During Occupy Boston, I met a PhD candidate studying social movements, Sophie. She had recently married an Egyptian activist named

Mustapha, who was an organizer during the Egyptian Revolution in early 2011. They were living in Cairo and invited me to visit, an offer I immediately accepted. The Arab Spring was one of the catalysts for Occupy Wall Street, and I wanted to learn about the community organizing that enabled their movement.

Pretty quickly, I had a few other pins on the map throughout the Middle East: a photojournalist friend in Turkey connected me with journalists and activists across Lebanon, Israel, and the West Bank of Palestine.

So this would be my trip: a few months in the Middle East and then almost half a year in India. In January 2013, I got on a plane in New York, and off I went. The first stop was Beirut, though the trip started with a hilarious snafu. I had a 12-hour layover in Moscow, and after spending the whole day in the airport, I was eager to finally get to my first stop. While waiting for the flight, I got into a spirited conversation with an American who was living in Beirut. We were facing away from the gate, and when we turned around seemingly a few minutes later, we were shocked to find the plane had left.

There was no calling it back, and they told us we had to wait for the next one, which wasn't until the following morning. So we spent that night trying to sleep on the cold, hard, metal benches of middle-of-winter Moscow airport. *What a way to start the trip of a lifetime*, I thought to myself. I was so excited by what was ahead that it was more funny than annoying. The next morning, I reached Beirut with a new friend and a great recommendation for a hostel to stay in, no less.

ENCOUNTERING THE MIDDLE EAST

Almost every day for the next eight months, I wandered to my heart's content, walking more than a dozen miles each day through broad streets, mountain paths, and crowded and colorful alleys. Those months roaming around Lebanon, Turkey, Egypt, Israel, Palestine, and Jordan were some of the most enlightening of my life.

With the privilege of brown skin, a male body, and a "perfect Californian accent" (according to someone I met), strangers seemed excited to open up to me. In Istanbul, my friend Ben, the younger brother of one of my best friends from college, shared his accounts of covering the biggest stories across the Middle East as a freelance photographer, from the Arab Spring to the Syrian War. (In the decade that ensued, this same Ben, Ben Solomon, went on to win Pulitzer and Emmy awards for his filmmaking and journalist work across the world.)

In Cairo, Mustapha and his friends gave fascinating and deeply personal accounts of the Egyptian Revolution. I learned about how basic yet extraordinarily difficult things fueled their success. For example, during the two and half weeks of the protests that ground commerce to a halt, residents of the city needed food and water. So, multiple working groups came together to tackle this problem as part of the planning for the marches.

The coordination to do this rested on the trust and relationships built between activist groups and the broader community, a process that took years. Groups from different backgrounds and with different agendas worked together, and that unity allowed for a clear expression of regime change. In just eighteen days, Hosni Mubarak resigned and fled, and 30 years of military dictatorship ended.

I let myself simply steep in these stories of courage, perseverance, and strategy. It was what my heart wanted to do, so I did it to my heart's content. I had absolutely no idea what I would ever do with what I was learning, and I wasn't interested in trying to figure it out. Day after day, enthusiasm and curiosity pulled me forward, and I just let it. The stories and experiences were lighting me up, and all I wanted was to keep doing things that connected me with my Inner World.

Along the way, I got a deeper sense of Islam and the role it plays in everyday life. The simple beauty of hearing the prayer call ring out across the various cities filled my heart with awe. While I am not Muslim, I experienced it as a sacred moment of mindfulness, a call to remember mortality, presence, and the fundamental preciousness of life. I wondered how many silly disagreements and how much unnecessary anger would simply dissolve in these moments, as the air filled with divine song. Putting aside the religious specifics, it seemed so obvious that this sort of regular pause in daily life would be beneficial to a society. I wish we had some non-denominational equivalent in the West.

While the trip was still in the beginning stages, I remember thinking that, already, I felt so grateful for the simple fact that *there are other ways to live.* The always-on, materialistic, sprinting-from-thing-to-thing vibe that seemed to rule the lives of everyone I knew back home was just gone, replaced by an urge to wander, marvel, and get lost, often at a snail's pace.

REDISCOVERING MY HOMELAND

As winter turned to spring in 2013, it was time for India. As far back as I can remember, the smell of the Indira Gandhi International Airport in New Delhi has carried with it an unparalleled feeling of home. This time, the feeling was even more pronounced, as I knew I would have a chance to soak up India in a way I never had before.

My primary intention was to explore Indian religion and Buddhism in particular. Seemingly since the beginning of time, Indian spiritual seekers and their variety of traditions – Hinduism, Buddhism, Islam, Jainism, Sikhism, and many more – have taken a here-and-now approach to the question of life and what it is. In their own ways, each has prioritized an open and direct perspective and method in exploring this question: presence, meditation, and finding the answers for oneself rather than relying on dogma or rigid ideas.

After spending a month and a half with family and friends around the country, I traveled to Dharamsala to attend the Dalai Lama's teaching on *The Guide to the Bodhisattva's Way of Life* (where I took the Bodhisattva Vow for the first time). The Dalai Lama started the teaching with a few lines that I'll never forget:

"I'm doing this teaching here in India for Indian people. The text of this teaching comes from the profound intelligence of an Indian master, Shantideva. While I am a Tibetan, the teaching represents *your* spiritual heritage, and you must make it your own in your practice."

Raised in a Western context for most of my life, being Indian had always been something extra, something that made me different. On this trip, I began to see my Indian-ness in a new light, to understand Zen training as a continuation of my heritage. The Buddha had lived and died in India, and Zen was the product of his teachings being carried through Northern India, China, and into Japan. My chosen spiritual path was an *indigenous* tradition, a living descendant of Indian spirituality. It grew out of the land and history of my homeland. In studying Zen, I was taking a piece of India and its spirit with me wherever I went.

RETREATING IN THE HIMALAYAS

After attending the teaching in Dharamsala, I wanted to find a monastery somewhere in the Himalayas where I could do a solo meditation retreat for a month or so. I took an overnight shared taxi to Leh, the main city in the desert plateau region of Ladakh. When day broke and I found myself in the midst of the Himalayas for the first time, my eyes filled with tears. I was overwhelmed by the beauty, bursting with gratitude and wonder at being in the presence of the mountains I had heard about my entire life.

On the advice of a fellow traveler, I made my way to a remote Ladakhi village called Lamayuru. For the next month, in a small dwelling above a mountaintop monastery nearby, I did my first meditation retreat. I had been practicing for about five years at that point, but mostly for around 30 minutes a day with the occasional half-day sit on a weekend morning.

This retreat was something different altogether. Each day, I awoke at 4am, hiked for 20 minutes up to the top of the mountain that the monastery was perched on, and did breathing exercises to warm up my body in the morning cold. I spent most of the day meditating, taking occasional breaks for yoga, tea, short hikes, and reading sections of *The Guide to the Bodhisattva's Way of Life*.

I felt the ebb and flow of practice. In some moments, I felt quiet, clear, and at peace. In others, a noisy mind led to feelings of hopelessness and futility. I watched faith and fear trade places like they were playing hopscotch, and, at times, just let it all be.

Up until this point on the trip, I had connected with my Inner World via experiences and adventures and seeing where and how I came alive within them. The retreat offered a different sort of Inner World connection. As I marinated in stillness, the awe and wonder I so often felt on the trip started to point inward. It wasn't just beautiful sunsets, endless ruins, and fascinating stories that I found wondrous, but the experience of my breathing body and the blood flowing through my veins.

My days were extraordinarily simple. Waking up, walking, stretching, and, mostly, meditating. The gong of the meal bell roused me from practice. The cold water cleaned my hands before each meal and my bowl afterward. Even the slight shortness of each breath at an altitude of 13,000 feet was comforting – reminding me, with a faint whisper, that I was alive.

TRUSTING OUR INNER WORLD

In Buddhist teaching, the opposite of the trance of unworthiness is called Buddha-nature. Buddha-nature is an inherent sense of worth, wholeness, and even perfection that arises from directly experiencing our human body. This wholeness has no reason or cause – we all possess and inhabit it inherently, without needing to do anything or be anyone else. The prolonged practice and stillness of retreat gave me a chance to encounter this teaching directly, to experience it in my own being. Day after day, I felt the simple magic of my alive body and the truth that everything, deep down, was *okay*.

This *okay*-ness is the revolution that transforms our relationship with our Inner World. The vast landscapes inside of us crave our companionship. Not in the form of thoughts or rumination or mindless introversion – they want our *attention*, our witnessing, our mindfulness. When we meet this desire, our universe changes. The need to fix ourselves drops away. Conditioning dissolves. Our Inner World grows comfortable asking for its needs directly. Healing flows on its own from the gentle awareness we're offering ourselves.

It's like building trust with a dear friend. At first, they might be careful about what they share or try to get their needs met without really telling you what's in their heart. But as you keep showing up, keep listening without judgment, they begin to open up more and more.

The key – and the trickiness – is staying present. Our trust with our Inner World – like in any friendship – must be constantly renewed. The memory of a best friend can be helpful, but it pales in comparison to the presence of them. If we want to be guided by our Inner World, we must continually establish our relationship with it in presence.

Ironically, this can make trust hard. When I started Athleague, I was super passionate about it. Later, as I kept deepening my presence and expanding my horizons, my connection with my Inner World grew stronger, but my enthusiasm ran out. This was *true* for me – it was the genuine progression of emotion – but that didn't make any it less jarring.

Retreat is so powerful because it forces us to see and *feel* the stuckness we might not have even known was there – and to move through it, back into our Buddha-nature and inner trust. Over time, our habit of looking outside of ourselves starts to atrophy, the trance of unworthiness drops away, and we grow into a relationship of trust and commitment with our whole life.

RETURNING HOME

It was a trip of a lifetime: wandering for miles through cities like Cairo and Istanbul, meeting fascinating people who were doing amazing things to make change in their communities, and engaging in spiritual practice in a remote monastery in the Himalayan mountains. Amidst it all, I was learning to trust my Inner World as a compass to navigate life, following the sense of Aliveness I felt flowing within me.

I returned to the US with the realization that our Western way of life is very small. In India, I felt liberation everywhere, from the quiet mornings in the mountains with the monks to the busy streets. While poverty is always painful, people who had far less than I did seemed to walk around more stress-free – *and happier* – than practically everyone I knew back home. So much of what we consider normal is the result of our culture and the specific forces that shape it.

The world around us defaults us into specific, Western ways of experiencing and moving through the world. But *there are other ways to live,* and on this trip, I got to *live* differently. In the years that followed, the memory of this trip was profoundly grounding. Whatever stresses and anxieties I was piling on top of my mind, somewhere out there was a rugged monastery overlooking a Ladakhi village, a quiet boat on the banks of the Nile, a crowded intersection in Delhi teeming with smells, sounds, sights, and, amidst it all, the relaxed gaits of people who looked like me.

My travels added fuel to the fire of Zen training – to explore and live the question of Aliveness. Despite not knowing what lay ahead, I felt clear, at ease, and deeply present as I landed back in the Bay Area.

10

DREAM CHASING IN THE BIG APPLE

I WAS full of energy and enthusiasm for what came next, but I had no idea what that was. And after a year of adventuring, I needed to start making money.

I was torn. On one hand, I was so alive with "let's change the world" energy and all the experiences I had with activist communities in the non-online world. And yet, I still felt drawn to technology as being a part of what I wanted to express in my work. What I really wanted was a job that did *both* — one where I could work on meaningful issues while I learned how to build software products.

This tension played center stage over the next three years, during which I was fortunate to work at two incredible organizations.

The first was Avaaz.org, a 100-person nonprofit that offered an online petitions platform (like Change.org and others) and campaigned for a variety of progressive causes around the globe, including human rights, climate change, and anti-war efforts. I was tasked with leading product innovation, brainstorming and building out new features on top of our core platform. It seemed like a perfect fit, and in spring 2014, I excitedly accepted and moved to New York City to begin my next chapter.

The work was meaningful. Shortly after joining, I got to be an intimate part of organizing the People's Climate March, then the largest climate demonstration in history. As an organization, our petitions would regularly garner millions of signatures and be a driving force in passing or blocking key legislation (mostly in Europe, Brazil, and Africa). But over the next year there, an uncomfortable truth started to become clear: the organization didn't want to prioritize new features.

I would create plans to pilot new ideas — like learning about new members via an onboarding flow — but we'd never have the engineering capacity to start building them. The day-to-day work was sucking up so much energy that forwarding-thinking investments were never deeply explored. By the halfway point of 2015, not feeling myself learning or growing, I decided to leave.

Next, I got a job as a product manager at the buzzed-about e-commerce startup, Warby Parker. In the mid-2010s, Warby Parker was known both as a prominent New York's tech startup *and* as a social impact success story: for each pair of glasses purchased, they would donate one to someone in need. It seemed like a perfect fit for my interests, combining both tech work and social good.

However, over the course of 2016, growth began to slow down significantly due to market saturation, and it became clear our projections for the next few years were far too optimistic. We stopped hiring new employees and postponed an IPO indefinitely (the company would not go public until 2021). Slowly but surely, Warby was losing its luster as an "It" startup in New York City, and people were beginning to leave.

On top of that, I saw from the inside how the social impact of the "buy one give one" program was limited at best. It was more of a marketing technique than a means of making a meaningful impact, and it was treated as such internally. I wasn't surprised, nor did I blame the company. But this reality was disheartening to see up close.

LESSONS FROM PRODUCT MANAGEMENT

There was, however, a silver lining to these two roles: I began to learn the craft of being a Product Manager. PMs, as they're called in the industry, set and execute on the product vision for software teams. This was essentially my primary role at Athleague, but being able to practice it both at a nonprofit and a tech startup, I got a wider perspective on what success looked like in varied environments.

Product management has two main competencies: understanding people and skillful execution. The first of these helps inform what needs to be built. PMs need to know how potential customers think, what really matters to them, and what they actually want (as opposed to what they say they want). Then, they take this knowledge and lay out a vision for a product that can solve customers' problems.

From there, PMs lead the building process, keeping their eyes on the big picture and making sure things run smoothly (technically, interpersonally, and everything in between). It's a dynamic, multi-faceted role, and I loved it (and still do). It's taught me to empathize deeply and understand what genuinely motivates someone, whether it's a user of a product I'm building or a team member I work with.

Above all, product management is rooted in the discipline of execution — how to do stuff *well*. In these roles, I deepened my understanding of frameworks and best practices that helped teams do just this, like Key Performance Indicators (KPIs) and Objectives and Key Results (OKRs). The details of these frameworks are less important than the heart of what they're about: *identifying and prioritizing what's important.*

Furthermore, this is approached as an *iterative* process. Product teams set goals and work towards them, checking in on progress via daily "standup meetings." Then, crucially, they regularly meet to reflect on how things went and brainstorm improvements. Over time, I saw how this process eliminated distractions, kept us on track, and catalyzed continual improvements in how we worked together.

FROM THE PRACTICAL TO THE SPIRITUAL

At my job, I was using these frameworks to help keep my teams focused and impactful, but I couldn't help but apply these perspectives to my life as a whole. The core problem any product team faces was the same core problem I felt myself facing in navigating life: understanding what's important and prioritizing it. I saw how the deathbed regret of "not living a life true to myself" was the macro flavor of the problem I was solving for my team at work each day, week, and quarter.

If my experiences in Occupy, Burning Man, and my backpacking trip began to lay the spiritual foundation for living a life true to myself, these frameworks were turning into the *practical* foundations for doing so. It would be years before I formalized them into the rituals that I'll share later in this book, but in an energetic way, they were already sharpening my focus. They were teaching me to look at my life through the lens of what's meaningful and how I could be more and more precise in making sure this stuff got prioritized in what I did and how I lived.

And in the "how I lived" part of the equation, Product Management had one more framework to offer me: habit loops (which we'll just call "loops"). Loops are a behavioral psychology concept popularized by Nir Eyal in his book *Hooked: How companies create habit-forming products.*

HABIT LOOPS

Here's a brief rundown of how habit loops work, using Instagram as an example since so many of us use it and return to it regularly on our own accord:

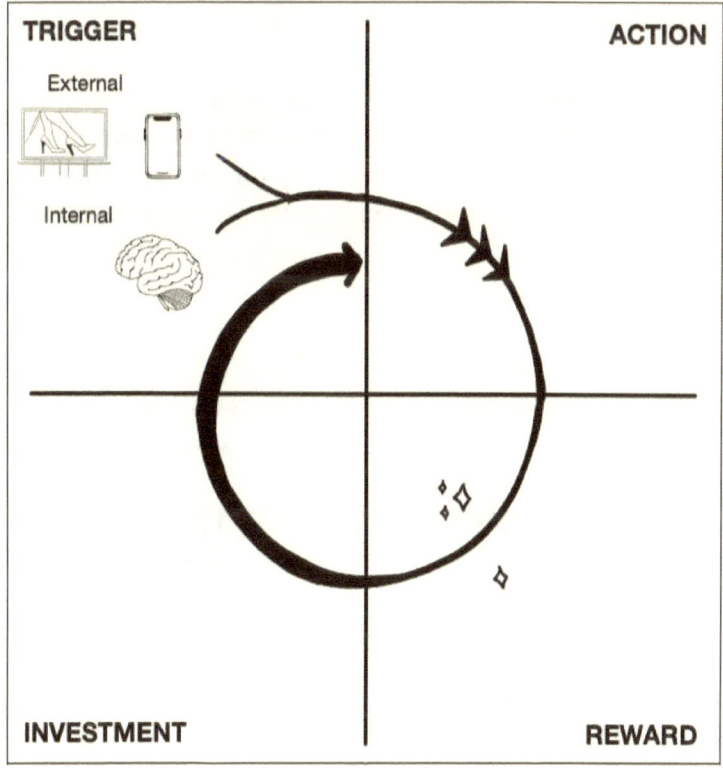

- Trigger: This is the thing that gets you to engage. In the case of a product like Instagram, it can be a notification that you got tagged on a photo (external trigger), or you had a moment of boredom and thought, "let me check Instagram" (internal trigger). Internal triggers are powerful because they've worked their way into our psychology — no one has to tell us to check Instagram; we just do it.

- Action: This is the thing we do. In the case of Instagram, we log on and start scrolling.
- Reward: We get some sort of pleasure or positive feedback. An example is seeing the photo we're tagged in. The more pleasurable or varied the reward, the more it creates a sense of longing or curiosity.
- Investment: We do things to strengthen the loop. We might like, comment, or post a story. Each of these gives Instagram more data and creates potential future triggers to pull us back into the product, like friends responding to a comment. As the icon alludes, investment leads to us getting more locked into the loop.

Loops are everywhere, and the framework can be applied to basically any habit, even daily occurrences like eating cookies. When I'm feeling anything from a sweet craving to a creeping sense of inadequacy (trigger), I reach for a cookie (action). It tastes great (reward), so when I go to the store, I buy more (investment). Cookies are almost too obvious a loop to mention, and yet loops like these model huge parts of how we actually live life.

In the most negative sense, loops describe addiction, and indeed, many tech companies (and companies of all stripes) are looking to get us addicted to their products. However, loops offer the simple insight that, when it comes to our habits, behaviors, and even ways of thinking and being, we're getting a reward and actively *investing* in them with what we do. Our most deeply internalized habits and ways of thinking carry momentum, power and sway over us based on how often we traverse their loop.

As a product manager, I was learning about how companies use loops to build products that get us hooked. But on a personal level, I became much more interested in how loops could be used to better understand how I engaged with my life. Loops, I discovered, were the means by which our lives got hijacked by the default world.

11

THE BRAIN ROT OF
DISTRACTION

WHEN I WAS BACKPACKING, I chose to take 18-hour bus and train rides to visit obscure ruins in Egypt or India at the drop of a hat. I'd revel in the slow travel — writing, reading, or doing nothing at all, not even thinking about my phone (there was never cell service anyway). Now in New York, I would get fidgety waiting just five minutes for the train to come, despite knowing I wanted to take this time to breathe and be present.

This erosion of my capacity for stillness felt like a symptom of something deeper. As my enthusiasm for work at Warby Parker dwindled, a sense of impatience, disconnection, and dissatisfaction started to show up everywhere. I'd notice my mind wandering during meetings and procrastinated my time away on Reddit. These patterns showed up in my meditation too — distracted thoughts seemed much more frequent. With the memory of ease and clarity from the backpacking trip still so fresh, the contrast between my mind now and how it felt back then was stark.

Looking back, I could tell you about how the origins of this had to do with my default world conditioning, how I was looking to my work for a sense of self worth. But I wasn't ready to go there. At the time, all I saw clearly was my distraction and the persistent sense of disquiet that seemed to follow me around. Zen had penetrated my bones enough that the usual methods of escape — going out, dating, stimulation in one form another — were not going to fix my ennui, though I occasionally tried.

So, I studied my angst. I saw how when I lost myself in distraction or activity, I was trying to escape the rudderless feeling that seemed to pervade my life. From Zen training, I knew I had found an entry-point, a pattern to move closer to. My attention was being drawn into activities, thought patterns, and habits that had greater pull over me than the simple experience of presence.

I found places where I did this habitually, like waiting for or riding the subway. These frequent, in-between life moments were the perfect place to take a closer look at my mind. I made it a practice to not take out my phone and answer emails and texts.

Instead, I focused on my mind and the thoughts that arose. I watched myself think, "I should respond to that text message" over and over again. In other moments, I just wanted to scroll social media and saw how my mind fixated on this thought with the same intensity.

I realized that it was less that I needed to respond to texts and more that I just craved input — *something* that I could bury my attention into. Non-stimulation was, at a basic level, deeply uncomfortable, and I would create whatever story or desire I needed to escape this discomfort.

One day, it clicked: this was a loop. Going through life, I'd encounter both everyday boredom and some flavor of listlessness, and either of these served as a trigger. With my phone in tow, I had the possibility of being able to take an action, whether it was responding to messages, scrolling social media, or anything else. This action carried a reward: I'd get something done or at least get a hit of dopamine while scrolling Instagram. Each time we choose distraction, it erodes our capacity to *pay attention*, which inevitably leads to more moments of discomfort, more triggers to draw us into this loop.

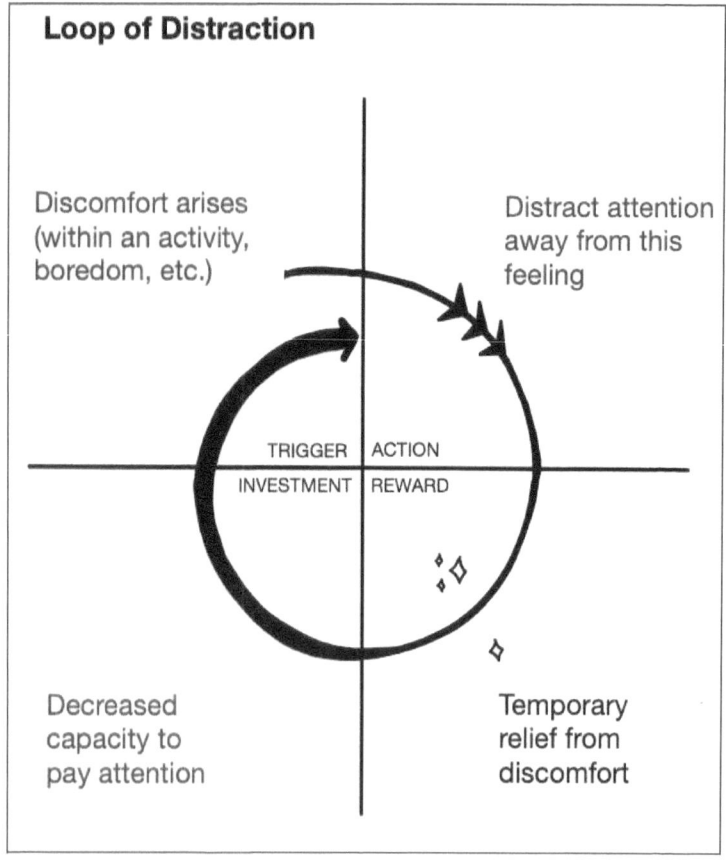

Loop of Distraction

Discomfort arises
(within an activity,
boredom, etc.)

Distract attention
away from this
feeling

TRIGGER | ACTION

INVESTMENT | REWARD

Decreased
capacity to
pay attention

Temporary
relief from
discomfort

I saw how the loop of distraction was directly opposed to Aliveness. When I simply sat with myself on the subway — when I chose to experience what I was feeling in my body instead of picking up my phone — the reward was centeredness and often insight as to what was going on inside of me.

Of course, distraction didn't just occur on the subway — I saw how I got distracted at work, with friends, even in romantic situations. Each of these moments had loops that started with some sort of discomfort. The sources of discomfort were vast — from the simple boredom of waiting for the subway to a sense of unease about the lack of purpose in my life to deep-rooted body insecurity in intimate situations — but the common thread was the basic desire to avoid discomfort.

When I followed that desire for avoidance, I saw how this loop — and the Inner World disconnection that came with it — further entrenched itself across my life. The sense of alleviation that the loop of distraction provided from discomfort was always short-lived, a hit of a drug that came with a hangover of anxiety and fidgetiness. Seeing this process within my lived experience was a game-changing moment, and as I would find, the rabbit hole of distraction went much, much deeper.

You know when you notice something and then start seeing it everywhere? That was me during my first couple of years in New York. I'd count the number of people glued to their screens on the subway. I noticed how often people would just drift off at work or while hanging out, their eyes glazing over and focus floating away (and the way this made me feel disconnected and unheard).

I was a little obsessed, but the obsession sharpened my reflections on living a true life. At the level of an individual day, we can get distracted away from a priority that we know is important to us. In the context of a meaningful project like building Athleague, my subconscious fear of failure and desire for validation distracted me away from making the necessary decisions to build a successful company.

Across our whole lives, one way of understanding "I wish I lived a life true to myself" is that we get distracted away from our truth. The moment-to-moment diversions lay the groundwork for the whole process, as daily behaviors become habits, habits turn into values, and these values work themselves into what we want to prioritize and who we are. The more I looked, the more I started to understand distraction as a silent killer and see how deep its rabbit hole went.

DISTRACTION MAKES THE UNHELPFUL ATTRACTIVE

Every time we, for example, distract ourselves with our screens, we're making a tradeoff: more stimulus but less *awareness*. Over time, our ability to pay attention narrows and erodes. We default to superficial forms of pleasure because we lose the capacity to feel and enjoy the deeper parts of life.

This loss of attention requires us to seek out more stimulation to feel anything at all. The more distracted we are, the more we, for example, gravitate towards unhealthy foods. We need their concentration of fat, sugar, and/or salt to *taste* something, to get the yummy feeling we naturally seek. The pleasure of a healthy, nutritious meal is subtle, and we're too distracted to enjoy it. In this way, we grow disconnected from the finer signals that our body is giving us. This pushes us to over-consume and makes it harder to cultivate a healthy lifestyle.

Finally, there's a social element to our brain rot. The sight of two people (or more) at a meal together on their phones has become disturbingly common. Genuine connection requires presence and being able to allow things like moments of awkwardness and silence. In our distraction, we're losing the ability to stay with one another through the natural ups and downs of our interactions. Heads buried in screens while hanging out makes sense: scrolling our phones has become more comfortable than the inherent uncertainty of meaningful relationship.

DISTRACTION FUNNELS OUR THIRST FOR ALIVENESS INTO ANXIETY

Let's say we want to play the guitar. In the process of learning to do so, we're going to encounter countless moments of difficulty, frustration, and discomfort. If our minds are too distracted, we'll turn away and, eventually, give up. In this way, whole possibilities for our lives become closed to us.

The consequences of this run deeper than we think. If playing the guitar is a true, deep wish of our Inner World and we can't honor it, the *energy* of that wanting turns on us. This energy is an intensity, a thirst for Aliveness. It *wants* expression.

Not getting it, this energy burrows its way into the minutia of our lives, trying to find fulfillment in other activities. We research (and stress out about) where we're going to eat like it holds the key to our soul's contentment. We obsess over Instagram activity as if our being loved is at stake. When the quality of our mind's attention is unable to steward our Aliveness, *our unfulfilled desire to feel alive turns into anxiety.*

This is just one pathway by which distraction leads to anxiety. At a fundamental level, if we can't pay attention to what's going on around us or inside us, we're going to feel perpetually unsafe! The anxiety isn't the problem, it's the symptom.

Depression and anxiety are epidemics in our society, and I believe that these conditions are primarily a cry for help coming from the deepest parts of our being. *We're not living life.* Our crisis is fundamentally spiritual and existential. In the times of my life that I've been anxious or depressed, this view has been extraordinarily useful. It's allowed me to not get caught in my mind's content but rather see these thoughts as a symptom of a spiritual thirst for *life*.

THE DEFAULT WORLD LOVES OUR DISTRACTION

Disconnected, anxious, and over-consuming are exactly where the default world wants us. In this state, we buy, post, and scroll at will. We turn the wheel of content, consumption, and materialism with our distracted energy. In doing so, we are freed for a fleeting moment from our discomfort. As this happens, companies sell things and make money, and we all have stuff to talk about, from the latest Netflix show to the last thing we bought.

It is, in fact, another loop. The distracted stuff we do gives us the reward of freeing us from discomfort for a brief moment, but it also rewards the people who make the distractions, allowing them to invest in making distractions more desirable and pervasive in our lives. In a superficial (and diabolical) sense, everyone wins.

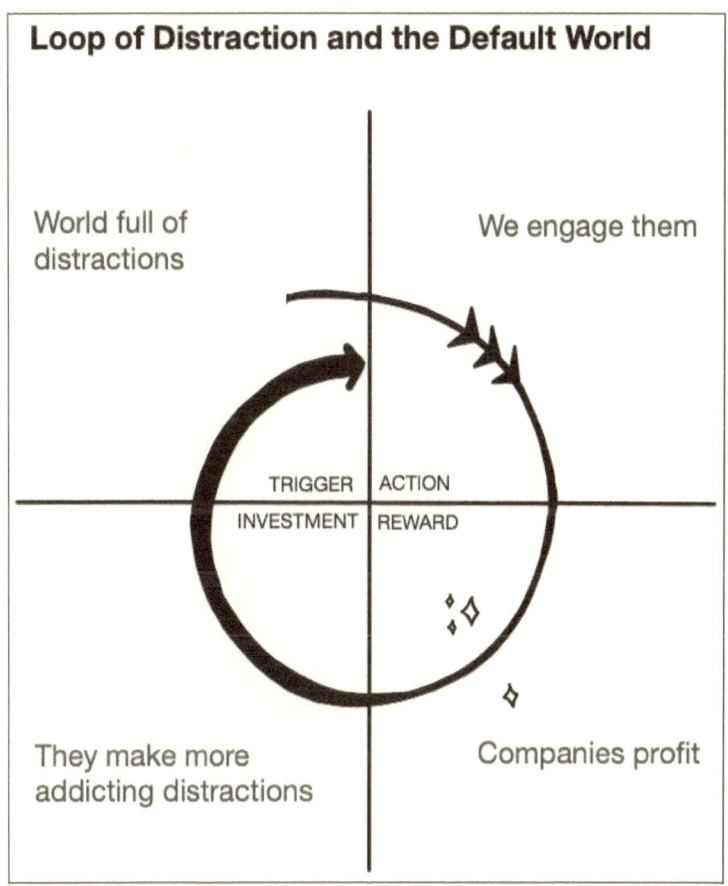

Loop of Distraction and the Default World

World full of distractions

We engage them

TRIGGER | ACTION
INVESTMENT | REWARD

They make more addicting distractions

Companies profit

Note: obviously, this isn't a habit loop. However, for me, loops have been helpful in understanding how momentum works in life and society and how cause and effect are so often intermingled.

The vast power of this loop can be depressing. I think that, deep down, most of us have built an identity around the consumption as a result of this loop. Whether it's of stuff, ideas, people, or merely social media, *we consume things as a way of trying to feel real, of knowing who we are*. In our distraction, we've lost the capacity to identify as simply being alive.

Day after day, as I rode the subway to work in the same Soho neighborhood where I had encountered that billboard years earlier, a chilling thought arose: we spend our whole lives in loops of distraction. Caught in the trance of unworthiness, it's one dead-eyed doom scroll to the next, from here until our deathbed, where we regret "not living a life true to ourselves."

MEDITATION RETREATS HAVE CONSEQUENCES

AFTER THE WONDER of my backpacking trip, the truth was hitting me like a ton of bricks: staying *alive* in the default world is hard. My response was to double down on my practice. I upped my daily meditation to 30-45 minutes, regularly read Buddhist books, and attended events and gatherings at Buddhist centers across the city. I even did a yearlong meditation teacher training in 2016.

As luck would have it, in the summer of that year, I moved to a new apartment in Brooklyn that was randomly and auspiciously across the street from Fire Lotus Temple, a Zen center affiliated with a monastery upstate called Zen Mountain Monastery (ZMM).

It felt like fate. Years later, I would realize that the handout on meditation instruction that I received from my college Zen professor was actually printed from the ZMM website. During my first visit to Fire Lotus Temple, I had an instant connection with the *sensei*, or teacher, who gave the Sunday talk, Ron Hogen Green. I started regularly attending Sunday gatherings. The following year, I formally joined as a training student with this same person, Hogen Sensei, as my teacher.

The ZMM community trained with a rigor and commitment I had never experienced before, offering meditation intensives and weeklong retreats every month. Hogen Sensei and the other teachers spoke openly about enlightenment — the radical experience of cutting through what I called the default world and living a true, awake life. "Realizing what the Buddha realized" was the clear, bald, unapologetic ambition, and the training reflected the vigor and dedication that this aspiration required.

Until this point in my life, Buddhism had been my deepest curiosity, a vehicle for living and experiencing life to the fullest. Over the course of 2016, it became an identity — a way of living within constant transformation. Two retreats I did that year were the pivot point of that process.

WHAT DOES IT MEAN TO BE A MAN?

Around the time I moved across the street from Fire Lotus Temple, a dear friend told me about an intriguing weekend retreat being hosted at the Brooklyn Zen Center (a different Zen center from my own but also nearby). It was entitled "Undoing Patriarchy and Unveiling the Sacred Masculine" and was led by two teachers I'd heard great things about, Kosen Greg Snyder and Lama Rod Owens. I signed up right away.

After an initial period of sitting meditation, the retreat started with a simple question: what does it mean to be a man? We split into pairs and were given ten minutes each to simply speak about our experiences, with one person sharing and the other listening without commenting or responding. Rather than thinking about our words, we were instructed to simply keep the prompt in mind and give voice to whatever came up. When one thought was finished, we returned to the question, sitting in silence until something else arose.

At first, my answers came fast and furious: the strength of my body, directness in my relationships with other men, the laid-back vibes of watching sports with my friends. I kept digging — re-answering the prompt — and similar themes arose in more nuanced forms: courage, play, and ease. I found my way to difficulties: A sense of responsibility to carry the load (literally and metaphorically), repression of sadness, and guilt around the ways gender-based oppression seemed to be everywhere.

Everything was both related to gender and, when I stayed with it, *not really about* being a man. In having to answer and re-answer the question, that one exercise revealed so many layers of both truth and hidden biases and beliefs. As we returned to the larger group to discuss what came up, themes like these and others emerged. Many men shared how they had a hard time feeling close to other men and developing intimate friendships where deeper feelings were shared. By the end, it was clear that all of us were carrying around subconscious masculine conditioning that affected how we lived and showed up in our relationships.

We explored our conditioning not with conversation but direct, embodied practice. An exercise later that day had us sit in chairs face to face with a partner with our legs touching. While sitting like this, we were instructed to give simple compliments to the other person while maintaining an awareness of how our bodies felt. It was wild to consciously experience our reactions in real-time. I was enjoying the closeness, but for other men in the room, the discomfort with touch and intimacy with another man was palpable.

UNDERSTANDING PATRIARCHY

Unworthiness and shame showed up throughout the process: not feeling like we could to take up space, be sad, or feel weak. I started to understand that this sort of conditioning was part of what kept me from opening up to people as it became clear that Athleague's market was too small. I didn't want to seem like a weak, failed man.

With this lens, a whole new empathy opened up within me for women and genderqueer folks. I thought about an older friend and her decades-long struggle with wanting to lose weight (after giving birth to two kids and going through menopause) and how this might be tied to default world conditioning she had received about what types of bodies have value and deserve love.

I began to understand patriarchy as an invisible but palpable force that caused female bodies vast suffering and violence for the entirety of human history — and one that pushed all of us into unworthiness (or conditional worth) via shame, objectification, body disconnection, and more

I emerged from the weekend a different person. I told people I loved them more often. I interrupted less. I stopped trying to fix situations and opened up to just listening and feeling empathy. I started to let myself feel sad more often, and shared it with people in my life. I felt myself more aware and compassionate, less needing to prove myself in situations that triggered me.

Beforehand, I could not have imagined the impact a single weekend retreat could have on me. Saying something like this is almost a cliche — but it's also completely radical and mind-blowing! That my understanding of *who I am* could shift so quickly and dramatically opened up a new dimension of what practice could be.

THAT THING THAT HAPPENED IN 2016

A few days after Halloween, I took a bus down to Baltimore to attend a weeklong meditation retreat led by Tara Brach and Larry Yang. None of us knew we were about to experience one of the most shocking moments in American political history.

The retreat had been planned months in advance and unintentionally coincided with Election Day. When we arrived, the organizers raised a practical question: should they post the results, or should we all wait until the retreat ended? The conversation felt almost casual. Fresh off the Access Hollywood tapes, a Trump presidency seemed impossible. Hillary Clinton's victory was assumed to be so certain that we simply decided to post the results in a side room. Those who wanted to know could check; others could wait until the end of the week.

You, uh, know what happened next. But knowing it now doesn't capture the physical shock of that moment. After 5 straight days of meditation practice, my body awareness was profound and deep — and this awareness felt my reaction to the news with starting clarity. During morning qigong practice right after I found out, my limbs jerked around involuntarily, no longer following my mind's instructions. It wasn't sadness or even fear — it was an outpouring of my whole being that defied a named emotion.

The first meditation period after the news broke remains seared in my memory. For 45 minutes, at least a quarter of the hundred participants sobbed openly. The sound was so overwhelming that a French participant, who hadn't yet heard the news, told me after the retreat ended he assumed there had been a natural disaster or terrorist attack.

When the period ended, Tara Brach took the mic. Her words captured our collective disorientation: "As most of you know by now, Trump won the election. I got the news this morning around 5am. I took a walk and cried, and now I'm here with you. We're all doing this live, and we have no playbook for this sort of situation. We're going to pause the retreat for at least the rest of this morning so we can process what's happened."

PROCESSING AS PRACTICE

Processing was *highly* necessary. My body was experiencing so much sensation. I let myself *feel* as much as I could, and as I stayed with it, I watched shock turn to anger and grief.

We split into small groups and took turns sharing how we were feeling, sitting quietly for a minute between each share. The silence gave us a chance to experience how our bodies were feeling as we moved between speaking and listening. Despite the sadness and rage, I felt an abiding sense of peace underneath the turbulence as we did this practice.

Morning turned to midday, and the teachers offered us forward-looking prompts: how would we respond? What was important to us now? What parts of our lives did we want to lean into?

I obviously didn't have a precise answer, but I sensed the morning's clarity of feeling being channeled into *resolve*. We had just elected a crass, ignorant, self-admitted predator as president. It felt clear that many people would suffer because of it. I wanted to *do something* about the situation we had found ourselves in and the forces that led us here.

We resumed the regular meditation schedule by the afternoon, and the retreat wrapped up on Friday of that week. To this day, I look back at the retreat with awe. The way we paused and explored our feelings left a lasting impression on me. If I hadn't been in that environment, I would certainly not have had the space and safety to explore the depth of my feelings as I processed the news. I would have avoided meeting the emotional energy that was stirred up, and that unfelt energy would have stayed in my body in the form of stuckness, clenching, grief, and anger.

Just a couple days after returning to Brooklyn, I knew I couldn't just work a regular tech job during this chapter of history. As I reconnected with the outside world and saw how many people were mobilizing, I felt myself deeply drawn to the energetic bubblings of resistance, wanting to find my place within it. Within a month, I left my job at Warby Parker after one of my best friends, Joshua, graciously offered me a part-time role leading digital product at his instant coffee e-commerce startup. Just like that, I had the financial and time flexibility to prioritize work I knew was important to me.

Now, I just had to figure out what that was.

13

RUNNING FOR MY LIFE

INAUGURATION DAY CAME FASTER than I thought possible, and the realities of the Trump regime were setting in: Muslim bans, deportations, border walls, the opening salvos of the war on women's bodies. It seemed the foundations of American civilization were shaking, shattering what had apparently been an illusion of sanity holding things together.

So much of my life and work had been rooted in an inherent optimism about our world, and this core pillar of my identity felt like it was crumbling. On top of this, I hadn't yet found an organization or idea to funnel my work energy into. As a result, the winter of 2017 was the most depressing period of my life.

My meditation practice was a haven, but I was finding that, on its own, something was missing. I consistently felt connected to my Inner World, but being present often seemed impossibly heavy — a debilitating mix of sadness, fear, and anger.

While I would not be able to put it into words until much later, I was starting to realize presence was not a static thing. I had been meditating for almost a decade at this point, and while I still encountered mental chatter and body discomfort while practicing, I could usually feel a deeper sense of peace underneath it all. I had assumed meditation was always going to be healing. Now, it occasionally felt unbearable.

Eventually, I stopped trying to stubbornly bear the heaviness and sought out new practices to augment my daily sitting. A friend recommended Haruki Murakami's *What I Talk About When I Talk About Running*, a memoir of the author's running journey. The book inspired me. I had always been an athlete and worked out almost daily, but I had never taken up running as a practice.

So in those first few days of the Trump presidency, I made a deal with myself: I would go on a run 6 days a week, but the only thing I needed to do was run one full lap around the block, which took less than 5 minutes. If I wanted to keep running afterwards, I'd do so, but only as long as it felt good. The consistency and lightness of the structure led to it quickly becoming a joyful routine — within a month, I was regularly doing 3-mile runs to nearby Fort Greene or Brooklyn Bridge Park.

NOT THROWING AWAY MY SHOT

That winter, I stumbled upon the soundtrack of *Hamilton*, the popular Broadway hip-hop musical about the life of Alexander Hamilton. I'd always been enamored by Revolutionary War history, and *Hamilton* fused a fresh historical take with one of my favorite types of music. With its epic stories of resistance, perseverance, love, and loss, the album struck a chord with me and instantly became one of my favorites.

A core refrain in many of the songs was Hamilton's determination to "not throw away [his] shot." The theme resonated deeply with me, as I felt this period of my life was an opportunity to do work and perhaps find a career that was infused with soul-level meaning.

One day, I put the soundtrack on as I went on one of my runs, and something came alive. The names of the famous heroes in these songs were the same names on the Brooklyn street signs all around me: George Washington, Nathaniel Greene, Horatio Gates, Baron DeKalb. Marquis de Lafayette, and more. So many of these figures' struggles and successes happened in the historic city I called home — some on the very ground on which I was running!

Things often felt hopeless, but during each run, Lin-Manuel Miranda (*Hamilton's* creator) reminded me of the hopelessness of a beleaguered, outnumbered, sometimes starving American Army endlessly running from the British. Our current moment was just one point in time, and across history, so many people risked so much for freedom and justice. Both of my cultural identities — Indian and American — included people who dedicated their lives to this struggle for liberation (both against the British, interestingly enough). Each time I got back home after one of these runs, my own despair didn't seem so impossibly large.

But perhaps the essential element was the cold. Even with long underwear, a thick sweatshirt, and gloves, the cold cut through to my bones, nearly overpowering me during the first few minutes of each run. Slowly, my body would warm up, but the cold was a constant companion, demanding my attention and mindful breathing.

This was the only way it could have been. In the face of persistent depression for the first time in my life, I *needed* to be uncomfortable, though I didn't quite know it at the time. The source of my pain was existential angst, and by taking on the challenge of cold runs, I was externalizing my angst, introducing a discomfort that I could then persevere through. In the process of staying present through it all, I was building back my capacity for simply being with how I was feeling. That rebuilt capacity *was* my healing.

I committed to these cold runs with a religious fervor, and they worked their magic. They gave me inspiration, exhilaration, and embodiment, and through the agency I was exercising within it all, I began to feel like myself again. Running through the Brooklyn winter, blasting *Hamilton* in my earphones — I wish I could say this was one of my cheesiest moments, but people who know me would say it's simply par for the course.

Aliveness, I was learning, was not just the simple peace of a long meditation session. It included freezing temperatures, the angst of my unfulfilled career dreams, and the suffering of so many people brought to the surface by political cruelty. Within it all, I was finding that I could trust the weird, cheesy, creative me-ness that guided me towards things like this quirky running practice.

14

AWAKENING

FROM THE TIME I had started practicing in Zen almost a decade prior, "mindfulness" had become a buzzword in pop culture. There were ads for the meditation app Headspace on the subway and meditation teachers leading practices in corporate offices (like Warby Parker when I worked there).

Given my background in tech, I was curious. I tried out the app, but its stress-reduction approach didn't resonate with me. The point of meditation, as I had experienced it, was *to be and feel alive*. Aliveness results in "less stress," but this seemed as silly as saying "love results in less stress." Certainly a true statement, but it completely misses the heart of the matter!

Worse, I knew firsthand that both meditating and being in love can, at times, be quite stressful. If I took a snapshot of a specific situation within a loving relationship or, of course, a particular period of meditation, I could very well conclude that both *increase* stress. If we're constantly measuring our practice (or our love) based on how quiet or anxious our minds are, we're going to be frequently disappointed.

As I saw it, Headspace and other apps like it were setting people up to fail with the false promise of stress relief. In contrast, whether it was exploring patriarchy, processing the election, or running through the Brooklyn cold, I was stumbling into ways of practicing that were helping me feel more and more *alive*. They were teaching me how to encounter my conditioning and feelings directly in my body. In the process, I was cracking open stuck ideas about *who I am* and moving into a larger, more fluid sense of identity.

And especially in those years, identity was everywhere. Between #MeToo and Black Lives Matter, large portions of society were feeling into previously suppressed rage in a very public way. It was an incredible time, but from what I saw, the ways this collective anger was being expressed more often led to backlash than genuine progress and broader empathy.

I realized my experiences, skills, and access to incredible teachers could be combined into a unique offering to meet the chaos and energies of that moment. At the retreat during the election, I saw how processing helped me channel sadness and anger into mission and resolve. At the retreat on undoing patriarchy, I uncovered a fresh, expansive sense of masculine identity that simultaneously deepened my awareness of and compassion for the impact of gender-related bias.

As a whole, Zen training was teaching me how to unwind the default world's impact on my psyche and come into alignment with my Inner World, and I wanted to share this possibility with others.

My next project was coming into clarity. If Headspace and others like it could succeed, maybe an app featuring the types of practice that had been so transformative for me could find an audience as well. And, of course, creating such an app would be the perfect project for me, combining my fierce drive to explore questions of spiritual liberation and activism with my professional experience in tech.

THE LIFE OF AN ENTREPRENEUR, ONCE AGAIN

I had a bearing, and it was time to start cranking. First, I needed to find some teachers to lead the meditation instruction portion of the app. I reached out to Lama Rod and Greg Snyder (who co-led the Undoing Patriarchy retreat), and they enthusiastically agreed to join. As it happened, Lama Rod had recently co-authored a best-selling book, *Radical Dharma,* alongside Zen teacher Rev. angel Kyodo williams (with contributions from Dr. Jasmine Syedullah). As queer and Black teachers, they explored the edges of Buddhist teaching as it pertained to their own lives, looking at patriarchy, racial justice, and queerness in a deeply personal compilation of essays and teachings. Lama Rod introduced me to Rev. angel, and she agreed to join our effort.

I was pumped to have these amazing teachers on board. I didn't know what the appetite for our type of product would be, but I figured if we could grow to just a hundredth the size of an app like Headspace, we could both build a financially sustainable organization and spread the perspectives and practices that had been so transformative.

I was optimistic, but I also remembered how my optimism had burned me with Athleague. I decided not to try to raise money from investors as I had previously done. Instead, I turned to Kickstarter to see if we could crowdfund our way to building the app.

After roping in a couple friends to help record a pitch video, we launched a $30k campaign titled "A new meditation app for breaking free from social programming." During the month of the campaign, I worked non-stop, emailing and texting everyone I knew and writing articles about our approach for prominent Buddhist magazines. At one point, I even stood on a street corner and talked to anyone who wanted to chat about our project.

It worked. With just a few days left and thanks to some large contributions from a couple friends, we ended up raising $34k. It was much less than what we raised with Athleague, but because I'd be working other jobs and investing my own savings, it was enough. I recruited engineering and design partners, and by summer 2017, we began building the app.

I called it Awaken (Buddhism literally translates to Awake-ism), and we modeled the design after popular apps like Headspace and Calm. The practices were inspired by the retreats that had been so powerful for me, a balance between investigating the socialized aspects of our identity and more basic meditations, intuitive movement and dance, stretching, and more.

Our teachers provided the major pieces of the content via meditation instruction, talks, and podcast-style conversations I had with them. For more basic mindfulness and movement exercises, I led some of them, and a friend from the meditation teacher training I did, Brooklyn-based artist Susan Stain-man, led the rest.

In many ways, our timing was perfect. Buddhist teaching offered a revolutionary way to explore the issues around identity and social systems that were swirling in the zeitgeist. In essence, our approach both acknowledged that these systems privilege some bodies over others but also were grounded in the reality that they harm everyone and block *all of us* from liberation. I had experienced this first hand during the Undoing Patriarchy retreat, feeling a profound sense of solidarity with people of all genders, rather than getting lost in guilt, blame, or avoidance, as most men do when it comes to patriarchy. My excitement was over the moon as our app's release date quickly approached.

GETTING AWAKEN OUT THERE

We launched the app in late 2017 and spent the next year building up the content library and user base. Given how deeply our work was speaking into the broader social movements of the time, it seemed like our app was everywhere, and sign-ups kept going up. By mid-2018, we had around 15,000 downloads, and I was attending and even speaking at a variety of events and finding myself in conversations with some of the most well-known teachers in the American Buddhist world.

The interest in the intersection of Buddhist practice and social activism seemed to only be increasing. On a frosty February morning in 2018, 300 Buddhists gathered at Union Theological Seminary in New York City to explore how the various *sanghas* around New York could do more collective action. One of our Awaken teachers, Rev. angel, gave the keynote, and it seemed like everyone there knew about our app.

I was on fire. My deepest interests — tech, activism, and Buddhist practice — had taken shape in a single project. It was like the sense of purpose that was Occupy Boston, of leadership and entrepreneurship that was Athleague, and my drive to discover the deepest parts of myself had merged into one. In addition, my work was deepening my practice, exposing me to new teachers and teachings that were expanding my horizons. I became a regular at the *Radical Dharma* retreats (led by Rev. angel and Lama Rod). They gave me a chance to explore race and my racial identity in the same way I had done with patriarchy, further opening up my world.

It blew my mind to feel the vast energy I had for the work, but it made sense: every retreat, every conversation, every new offering we released was feeding not just Awaken but my own journey of awakening. It was all part of my practice; I found myself pouring every bit of my being into the work.

15

THE LOOP OF BUSYNESS

ONE AFTERNOON IN LATE 2017, as I hammered out an email with my head and neck crammed into my phone while walking up my block on State Street in Brooklyn, I literally almost ran into my Zen teacher, Hogen Sensei, and his wife.

I was mortified. I can still see the piercing look he gave me as our eyes met. It spoke volumes without saying a single word: what in the world was I doing? Amidst this breakneck pace, where was my mindfulness, my practice? It triggered a more fundamental question inside of me: I was working on something I passionately cared about, but *did I actually want this life?*

Realization dawned: My busyness was wrecking me. I was putting my life energy into Awaken, desperate to make it work. On top of that, I freelanced as a product consultant to pay the bills. Wanting to escape it all, I'd pack my weekends with activity, so much so that I found myself constantly running the half block from my apartment to the Zen center because I was always late for practice or gatherings there.

It had become a self-perpetuating cycle. I was squeezing and wrenching my life force into trying to make Awaken success-ful. *It was my shot*, and I didn't want to throw it away. But in the process, I was putting an enormous pressure on myself. The only way I knew how to deal with the energy was to channel into non-stop work. But this had made my life anxi-ety-producing, exhausting, and less mindful. I wanted more time for rest, which meant, in my logic, that I needed to find ways to work faster.

Like so many others, I turned to the world of productivity. Between 2017 and 2018, I devoured dozens of books, articles, and videos on frameworks and approaches to getting more done. Getting Things Done (GTD), the Pomodoro Technique, Tiago Forte's CODE (Clarify, Organize, Distill, Engage), and many others — I did it all. This gave my chaos an organized feel, and for more than a year, they helped me control and manage my busy life.

And yet, even as I enacted these productivity hacks, my life didn't *feel* less busy. My orientation towards my time and energy didn't change — I just had new strategies for how I could load up my schedule and *do* as much as possible.

I was treating the symptoms but not the root of what was going on, chasing productivity as a solution rather than understanding it as *a co-enabling factor* of my busyness. The core value of productivity is efficiency, and when I valued it, I took on the *mind* of efficiency. I started to turn my time and, eventually, my whole life into puzzle pieces to be produc-tively pieced together. In the process, I was losing touch with the magic of doing things for the enjoyment and pleasure of *just doing them*.

Especially in a place like New York, my busyness was constantly socially reinforced. When I shared how overwhelming my life felt, my friends would all empathetically nod and tell me they understood because, of course, they were struggling with overwhelm too. My response to being worn out by the hamster wheel was to try to run faster, and this had become a core way I navigated life. I had, in fact, discovered another loop:

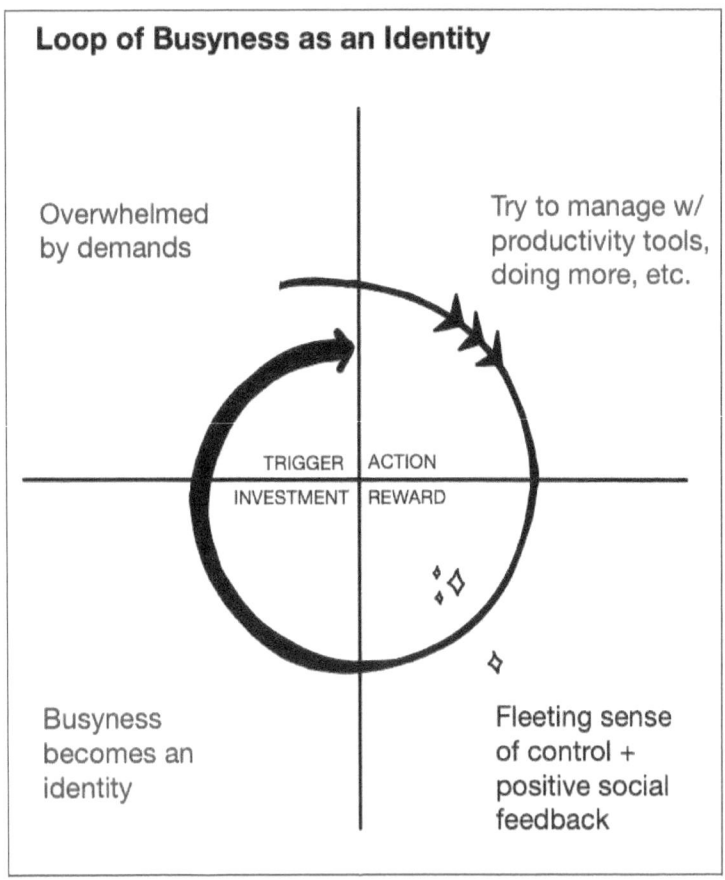

Loop of Busyness as an Identity

Overwhelmed by demands

Try to manage w/ productivity tools, doing more, etc.

TRIGGER | ACTION
INVESTMENT | REWARD

Busyness becomes an identity

Fleeting sense of control + positive social feedback

THE PRISON OF BUSYNESS

Eventually, the exhaustion of the busyness loop began catching up to me. I grew scattered and less strategic in my work, picking things to focus on that were less impactful but cognitively simpler.

I noticed how often I'd procrastinate, habitually opening up Reddit in moments of frustration and fatigue. I felt stupid doing this, and this feeling drove me to try to work harder, quickly creating a situation in which I was perpetually unsatisfied. If I was productive and humming along, I'd just keep working to get more done. If I wasn't getting much done, which was increasingly the case, I'd keep working out of shame and despair.

I saw these cycles and tried to fight them. I went on meditation retreats, scheduled time for self-care, and pulled back from an overactive social life. These worked in the short term, but when I got back into my daily life, momentum slowly but surely pulled me back into the loop of busyness.

I realized the depth of the impact of busyness as an *identity*, how it was distraction in the form of a lifestyle. The overloaded life is attractive to us because it's an outlet for our anxiety, a way to channel our avoidance of discomfort into something that the default world tells us is positive: *doing* things.

Busyness has become a badge of honor, a status symbol. At work, the people "at the top" are the busiest — a sign that, surely, their time is the most valuable. Outside of it, so many people (especially extroverts) feel deep resistance and even shame when they have an empty social calendar.

We come to feel our sense of worth depends on our staying busy and *doing* things. This "doing" can take many forms. We can pack our schedules, as I did when I was working on Awaken. More subtly, our penchant for needing to sustain activity can penetrate our inner psyche. Busyness no longer stays in the realm of a packed schedule, but starts to manifest as a mind that can't just *be*, whether it's via non-stop thinking, endless content consumption, texting and social media, or anything else. In this way, the most introverted people who rarely go out can have lives that feel frantic.

Over time, our basic okayness starts to hinge on keeping this doing-life going. Slowing down is not valued within the identity box we've created for ourselves; we grow increasingly uncomfortable feeling worthy and okay just *being*. Tara Brach names busyness as a symptom of the trance of unworthiness in the very first chapter of her book, and I was seeing it firsthand as I worked on Awaken. I ping-ponged between speeding up and slowing down because, while it helped temporarily to do less, I was still stuck in the prison of busyness as an identity, as a way of feeling a sense of worthiness.

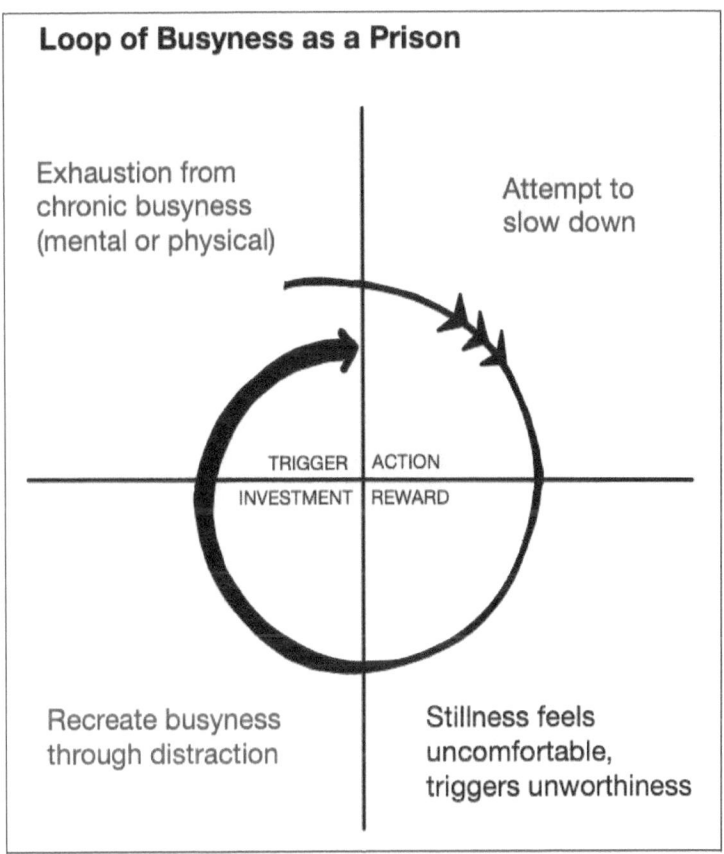

Note: this "reward" clearly is not a positive thing that encourages us to take the action of trying to down. However, it's the result when we're caught in the loop of busyness as a prison. We keep trying to slow down without intentionally building our capacity to be with slowness via mindfulness practice of some sort, so we stay stuck in the loop. Similar dynamics occur in any loop that we can't shake in which the "reward" isn't positive.

Seeing this dynamic in myself, realization dawned — my busyness was wrecking me. In the process of trying to make an app offering radical presence, I was losing touch with my own.

I needed to shift my conditioning — to sniff out the moments when I was speeding up and ceding my sense of self-worth to *doing*. I wanted to use those moments to pause, breathe, and allow myself to just be.

I did everything I could to interrupt my patterns. I put reminders in my calendar to breathe, take breaks, and go on walks throughout the day. I gave myself visual cues and rituals, like lighting a candle when I worked and blowing it out when I was going to step away from my desk for a while. Tried as I did, though, I couldn't stick to habits of slowness, reflection, and prioritization.

Finally, I hit a wall. I admitted to myself that I couldn't do this on my own. I needed help.

FROM MADNESS TO METHOD

Using standups from product management as inspiration, I posted a position on a freelancing website for a "morning coach." My thinking was that I wanted to get really good at prioritizing what I was going to do each day. By planning my priorities with someone and then having to report back the following day as to how it went, I would create a natural feedback loop. I could only say I was going to do 10 things and then not do them a certain number of times before I'd feel like an idiot doing so. I'd be forced to start getting real with myself about my work capacity. What I wanted was someone who could simply show up, hold me accountable, and help me see my patterns.

A few brave souls responded to the ad, and one person in particular, Caro, stood out. A dancer and freelancer living in Medellin, Colombia, she was the perfect combination of organized and alive with life. She was also doing this type of remote work to save up for a world-traveling backpacking trip, which seemed like a good omen.

Caro changed the game for me, making it easier to be more intentional with my energy every day. We met for 15 minutes each morning, and I made sure I was getting these 15 minutes right. By clearly delineating what was important and not, I could focus on the meaningful stuff. In doing so, I created a container to hold my work life and, increasingly, my *life* life.

Each week, I set three work goals as well as an intention or desired vibe for each week — a word or phrase that pointed to how I wanted to feel. No matter how discombobulated I got during the week, I could pull up my list each morning and know exactly what I wanted to focus on. On top of that, simply bringing to mind the vibe I had selected helped me stay more centered amidst the ups and downs of the day.

Over time, having these strict boundaries allowed me to better gauge my capacity. I began to end each day with a clearer and more consistent feeling of "done" rather than scrambling to do more. The busyness loop started to dissolve, and I felt the return of some of the spaciousness and presence that had so defined my backpacking trip.

When Caro found a job that made our regular meeting time infeasible, I got an email from a recent college graduate with a background in Buddhism and social justice, Emmye Vernet, who was enthusiastic about Awaken and interested in helping.

Under Emmye's brilliance and guidance, we took the system to the next level, formalizing many of its elements and dreaming up many of the principles, practices, and rituals you'll read in the coming sections. (And in case that name looks familiar, this same Emmye is the editor of this book.)

SAYING GOODBYE TO ALL THAT

For most of 2018, leading Awaken was a dream. With my life being held by the rituals of pausing and articulating what was important, I was thriving. But as 2019 rolled around, it was clear Awaken wasn't. Our active user count had gone down since our summer 2018 peak, and we weren't attracting or retaining paid users long enough to make a financially sustainable business.

I attributed this to two reasons. First, with the growth of our teachers' popularity, it became harder to record new material. We launched with the idea that Awaken would offer a unique, step-wise curriculum. With our teachers now traveling around the globe giving talks and holding retreats, this became harder. I was too slow to realize this and recruit new teachers into our community.

The second reason ended up eclipsing the first — the market was just too crowded. Meditation apps had been around awhile, and even with our innovative approach, we were chasing the wave, not riding it. None of the meditation apps that launched around when we did had much success in building businesses.

By early 2020, I decided to close up shop. We put the most popular practices and teachings into a podcast and shut down the app. It was sad — I had really hoped *this would be it* in terms of finding purposeful work. It brought up feelings of the lostness I felt when Athleague, Avaaz, or Warby Parker didn't work out. Around this time, a relationship I had been in for 4 years was dissolving, which brought its own challenges and heartbreak.

I knew that I needed a change. It was time to move home to the Bay Area. That summer, my friend Joshua wound down his coffee startup and took a product management role at

Google. He needed a break from passion projects and, perceiving that I could use one as well, nudged me to apply to product jobs. I had never worked in big tech, and given my anti-establishment orientation, I was pretty sure I wouldn't like it. And yet I found myself curious: what could I learn working at one of these influential companies, and what might that lifestyle be like?

I wasn't naive. I had been thoroughly disabused of the notion that the tech industry was somehow a magically positive thing for society. But the reasons for just applying and seeing what happened started to add up.

For starters, Joshua was right — I was exhausted. I was open to the idea that maybe I didn't need to prioritize impact and passion in my work quite so much. I figured a regular job would give me space to both focus on Zen practice and develop the life prioritization methods I had been prototyping into something I could share with others. Beyond that, working in tech would allow me to afford life in the Bay Area.

I applied to some open roles and eventually got a few offers, including one from the e-commerce platform Shopify. I asked my sister, who worked in the industry, about the company. She replied, "Working for Shopify right now might be like working for Google in the mid-2000s. They're one of the hottest companies around." Convinced by her conviction, I accepted the offer in early 2021.

16

FINDING AND LEAVING BIG TECH IN SILICON VALLEY

JUST LIKE THAT, I was working in big tech. As my sister had mentioned, it was indeed a good time to be joining Shopify. The company's primary product is a platform to sell things online (as an independent store, not a listing in Amazon's vast catalog). Given the pandemic, retail businesses were moving their operations to the internet, and most of these businesses were choosing Shopify to power that transition. As a result, the company had a banner year in 2020, riding the pandemic-fueled e-commerce trend to all-time highs in customer base, revenue, and stock price.

I joined with enthusiasm. At Shopify, I could just do my job and live my life — and my savings account would increase in the process! Going into the role, I was committed to a strong work-life balance where I could dedicate more time to meditation and Buddhist practice, my friends and family in the Bay Area, and a sweet new relationship that was taking shape.

Things were ramping slowly until, a month into my time there, my manager was fired just a few weeks after returning from paternity leave, and I was asked to lead his team. It was jarring. This person had just hired me! I hadn't been given any warning that this was happening. I was intrigued by the idea of leading a big team, but the way it happened felt cold and disorienting.

There was no time to pause and sort out my feelings (there never is in the corporate world). I was thrown into my new reality, with most of my colleagues telling me that this was "an amazing opportunity." Here I was, brand new to the company, and I had a whole team of my own to lead and the chance to make a name for myself. From the default professional perspective, it was a dream come true.

Compelled forward by various factors — professional opportunity, a chance to practice leadership, and a situation that allowed me to deepen my new coworker relationships — I dove into the work headfirst. "Work-life balance" quickly went out the window.

At first, I was enlivened by all of it. By making simple changes that improved the user experience, our team had more success in the first three months than the product had experienced in the previous three years. I could feel my team's trust in me, and I loved how the opportunity gave me a chance to channel my natural social gifts and extroversion into leadership. More importantly, our team was clearly having fun and enjoying each other's company.

Within six months, I was asked to create a two-year roadmap and present it to senior management, a stamp of approval from the higher-ups. I worked nights and weekends to do deep strategy thinking and came up with a vision that I had a ton of confidence in. When they heartily approved the plan I laid out, it felt like a major validation of my effort and our team's progress. I was working hard, but between our success and the close relationships I was forming with my team, I was actually loving the job.

THE UNDERBELLY

Just a couple weeks later, those same higher-ups announced our product was going to be shut down, alongside a bunch of other changes in our division (called a reorganization, or "reorg"). It was my first real taste of corporate life. Personally, I was going to be fine — I was reassigned to lead the biggest product in our group — but my work and our product's progress were all gone, just like that. I felt hollow and misled.

The new role was glamorous for a hot second. I remember being in a meeting with the CEO of the company and thinking: *wow, I guess this is cool.*

I soon found out it wasn't. Making minute changes now required multiple meetings with stakeholders who had their own personal agendas. I was now mired in constant politics, which made genuine teamwork difficult and required me to constantly be on my guard.

As I struggled to find motivation within the corporate slog, I had to acknowledge the obvious: I didn't care about any of this. The company, a potential promotion, the impact of our work — none of it was personally meaningful. I had mistaken the mountain of positive feedback of the first few months for Aliveness. My new, post-reorg reality was the cold water that doused me awake.

With my eyes now open, I started to make out how seductive the whole game was. Promotions and landing influential projects served as worthiness scoreboards. Compensation and benefits allowed for personal indulgence and the promise of financial ease. Corporate culture reinforced that this whole thing mattered and was real.

I wouldn't end up leaving until I got laid off (more on that later), but with this clarity in place, I reflected on what exactly had happened inside of me — how I had gotten sucked in and what it meant for what was next.

THE NUMBNESS OF PROFESSIONAL LIFE

What Shopify granted me was a window into modern professional life — the lives that many of my friends had been leading for a very long time. Few, if any, of these friends seemed happy or particularly *alive*. I had often wondered why so many seemingly intelligent people worked at jobs they so clearly didn't like. Now, I could explore why I had done the same.

The obvious answer is money, and tech companies indeed pay great salaries. However, the people who work there rarely cite their salary as the most meaningful part of their jobs. Instead, people at Shopify would talk about their "passion for the mission" (which at Shopify included "helping entrepreneurs" and "making commerce better for everyone").

The company worked to instill this passion. While on a business trip to Vancouver in 2022, the company organized a tour of a local macaron bakery. The bakery had signed up for Shopify during the pandemic, and our product allowed them to move to a delivery model with online checkout, helping them not just stay in business but grow. As in-store shopping resumed, they even opened a second location on the other side of town.

The story genuinely warmed my heart. I identified as an entrepreneur, and I wanted to believe Shopify was doing a good thing in the world. So, consciously and unconsciously, I tried to convince myself of this, to cultivate "passion for the mission." I talked about stories like these with my friends and listened to an internal podcast that played up our positive impact.

However, I also noticed another part of me, a quiet voice that realized how silly this all was. Shopify, like all e-commerce companies, is fueling widespread consumption of mostly worthless crap being produced and shipped all over the globe — sucking up natural resources and burning fossil fuels in the process. Sociopolitically, I was under no impression we were a positive force in society.

I knew all this, but I still wanted to believe. It was more than a want, actually — it was a need. In order to show up every morning, I needed to believe in our positive impact in order to feel interest in my work. The sober, reality voice that was countering my mental gymnastics had to be pushed aside. I wasn't fully aware this was happening in real-time, but after the reorg, it started to become clear.

I was doing the best I could to make a situation work, and I don't think I was the only one. In the end, I don't regret trying to work at Shopify. It helped me peel back yet another layer of our default world.

THE LOOP OF NUMBNESS

My attempts at self-deception were one piece of a larger dynamic enabled by professional life: numbness, a type of distraction that blanketed over my entire life. It was the final piece of the puzzle in my understanding of why we don't live life *alive*.

The only way I could have the energy to work was by numbing myself to my inner truths. This numbing created an angst within my being. My Inner World was telling me *this didn't matter*; my conscious mind was ignoring this and trying to convince myself of the opposite.

This angst followed me when I wasn't working, creating an energy I needed to continue to avoid. And lo and behold, when I got off work, there was my tech salary, ready to enable me to consume my way out of my feelings. I would eat out when I was too busy to cook, take gym classes to stay healthy, and hit the local *banya* (Russian-style saunas) to unwind — all without worrying about the cost. My consumption had the veneer of being non-materialistic, so I had a hard time seeing it for what it was: a way of avoiding my Inner World and its messages about my life. It was another loop:

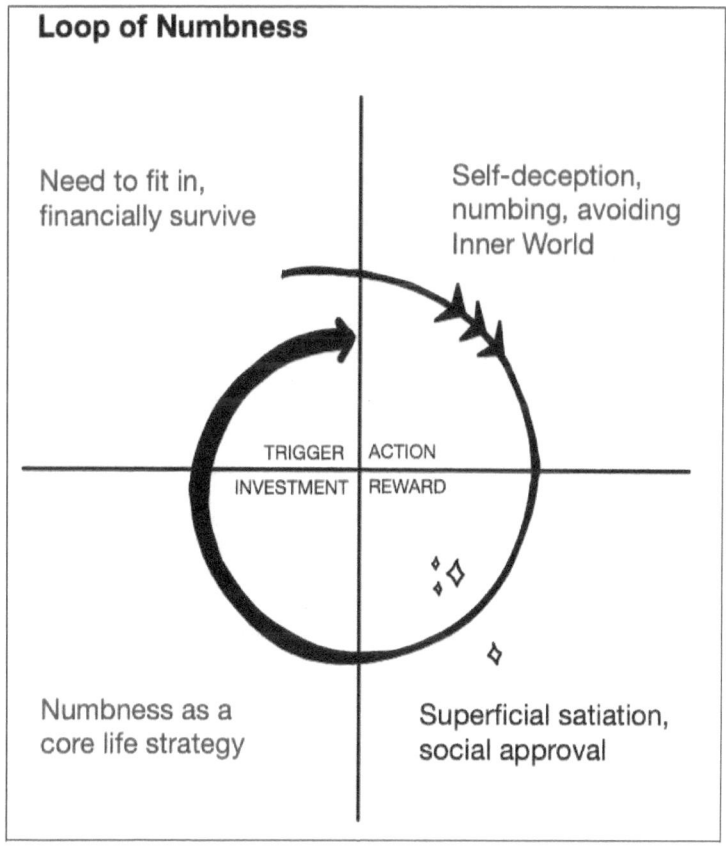

Loop of Numbness

Need to fit in, financially survive

Self-deception, numbing, avoiding Inner World

TRIGGER | ACTION

INVESTMENT | REWARD

Numbness as a core life strategy

Superficial satiation, social approval

I had unlocked a whole lifestyle, one that guaranteed a particular sort of comfort but demanded my numbness and self-deception. If I stopped to question my commitment to work or whether consumption was really making me happy, the whole thing would fall apart.

I now understood why my friends working mainstream jobs would sometimes react so forcefully when I used to question the impact that certain companies and industries were having on the world. For most people in corporate employment, this loop of numbness is the source of our energy; *it powers our lives.* To inquire into it is to threaten the very source of our livelihood. Turning inwards would disrupt the loop and thus is thoroughly unsafe, so we don't do it.

But deep down, I think we all want to care about the contents of our lives, and that includes our jobs. While I worked at Shopify, I saw how this desire to care would elbow its way into my consciousness, trying so hard to find satisfaction and meaning in other parts of my life that it turned into anxiety.

My energy ping-ponged between these two forces. Caught in the loop of numbness, I was relying on *not feeling* as a strategy to navigate work. But not feeling made it harder to satiate my desire to *live.* I'd project the angst that resulted from this into the rest of my life – from small decisions like where to eat to big ones like what to do about a romantic relationship. It was like I needed something to chew on, and that chewing could be fruitful and life-giving (in the midst of deeply enlivening work, for example) or pointless and anxiety-inducing. It was another loop:

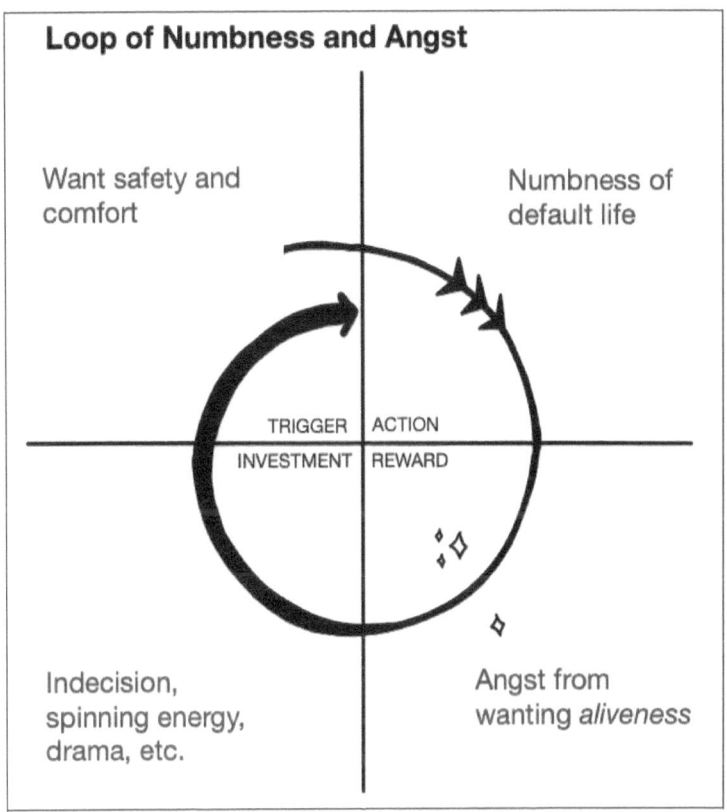

Within these loops of numbness, our bodies and depths are not felt, and our minds get hooked into anxiety. We're increasingly disconnected from the life of our Inner World. By retreating to the world of dissociation, plans, and consumption, we turn the volume of life down. It's not just that we're not living a life true to ourselves — we're dying, little by little, exhausting our life energy in keeping these loops spinning every day.

17

THIS PAINFUL DEFAULT LIFE

As the pandemic abated in late 2021, I finally had the opportunity to go on *sesshin*, a traditional week-long silent meditation retreat in the Zen tradition, at Zen Mountain Monastery. I had been doing two or three *sesshins* a year since 2016 but hadn't been able to go while everything was shut down.

During the first couple days, as I dropped my worries, stories, and habitual patterns in the silence and space of intensive retreat, my entire experience of meditation was *pain*. I was face-to-face with what had been under my numbness all along.

It was concentrated in my neck and shoulders but occasionally showed up in other parts of my body — hips, knees, heart. On the cushion and off it, I carried a feeling of general tightness and constriction, with electrical sensations emerging as my awareness settled in those locations of my body. At times, it felt like torture.

What's going on here? It can be tempting to blame meditation for this. During *sesshin*, we're on the meditation cushion for more than 10 hours each day. There is a very easy story I could tell myself that this much time sitting in stillness was the cause of my pain.

But I don't think that's what was going on. This pattern of pain being prominent at the beginning of *sesshin* was something I had felt before, though it was more intense during this retreat. But just like it had done previously, after the first day or two, the pain faded.

As far as I can tell, this initial period of aching is my mind coming into contact with the sensations that have been present in my body but ignored by my awareness — un-numbing, essentially. This pain is present in everyday life, but outside of moments spent in meditation or yoga, I'm usually moving too fast to feel it. When I land in retreat at the monastery, the floodgates open, and I'm able to perceive what my life and its habitual patterns *actually* feel like.

I believe we all carry this pain. It's the physical pain of sitting, crouching, hunching, whether it's over our desks, on our phones, or anything else. It's the unfelt emotional discomfort of our lives, avoided through stimulation and distraction. It's the existential angst of not living a life true to ourselves.

This pain is the multilayered anguish of our being, which only fuels our desperation to avoid it. To feel it in its fullness within everyday life would be too much, or so we subconsciously think. Its potency overwhelms our capacity for feeling, and we *stop feeling* — we numb ourselves — as a fundamental strategy for coping with life. And yet the pain *wants* to be felt, so it expresses itself in a myriad of ways: body pain, stress, anxiety, depression, and more.

When on *sesshin*, I encounter this pain directly, and it eventually washes over and through me into realization and Aliveness. The time and space I have to *feel* my body and heart are a large part of why I emerge from retreat so refreshed, even if the activity itself is so challenging.

DEFAULT LIFE IN THE DEFAULT WORLD

Distraction, busyness, numbness, drama — these are examples of some of the loops that run our lives in the default world. Whether in our love lives, at work, or in our friend groups, loops like these are all grounded in the trance of unworthiness. They cause us to run away from significant others or jobs when they get uncomfortable and feel forever unsatisfied. Conversely, we can run from the discomfort of *leaving* a job or partner and stay in an unhealthy work situation or relationship for years. We might shy away from the discomfort of authenticity with our friends and then feel unfulfilled in our connection with them.

Our specific versions of these loops may vary, but they all stay in place with a lifestyle of distraction that inevitably depletes our capacity for attention, worthiness, and vulnerability. We chase the superficial, and our deeper drives will remain wanting. The energy of that wanting looms large, turning on us in the form of chronic pain and anxiety.

The default world is *always* encouraging this. It chews up our life energy and spits out anxious, numb, dissociated lives, desperate to consume what it's offering us as an escape. Our desires for community, acceptance, and expression turn into Instagram posts, follows, and likes. Our yearning for love gets swallowed by Tinder's endless fish in the sea or trying to buy the perfect thing to feel attractive.

In Buddhist cosmology, there is a realm of existence inhabited by "hungry ghosts," beings characterized by large mouths and long, thin throats. These ghosts have vast appetites, but everything they try to eat or drink can never make it down into their bellies, so they never feel fulfilled or satiated. Their state of being has eroded to the point where satiation is beyond their capability. They forever crave more and are forever unsatisfied.

We are hungry ghosts within the default world. The stimulation we're devouring is toxic, poisoning how we live and our core beliefs about who we are. Over time, we get sucked into distraction not just by habit, but as a lifestyle. Entranced in this loop, we lose the ability to not only be nourished, but to even *recognize* nourishment. Instagram and Netflix are how we unwind. Junk food is where we go for comfort. The default world's traps are our solace.

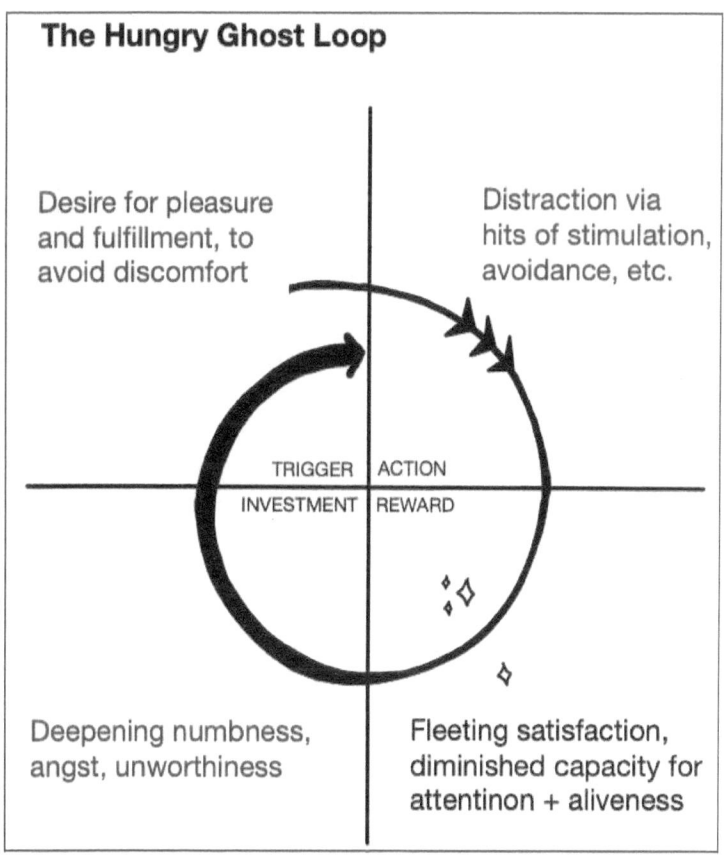

The Hungry Ghost Loop

Desire for pleasure and fulfillment, to avoid discomfort

Distraction via hits of stimulation, avoidance, etc.

TRIGGER | ACTION

INVESTMENT | REWARD

Deepening numbness, angst, unworthiness

Fleeting satisfaction, diminished capacity for attentinon + aliveness

The hungry ghost loop essentially encapsulates all the loops we've looked at so far. Do you feel how its logic is almost beautifully self-contained? In temporarily trying to abate ourselves of discomfort, we find ourselves more deeply trapped within the default world's web, a prison steadily robbing us of our capacity for attention, presence, and genuine enjoyment — and making us ever thirstier for ways to escape discomfort into distracted pleasure.

So, how do we untie this knot? As famed Buddhist teacher and activist Thích Nhất Hạnh says, "The way out is in." That is, to find our way out of this mess, we must turn inward. The hungry ghost loop runs on our habitual outward orientation, the myriad ways in which our attention is consistently pulled away from our experience and into distraction and preoccupation. We need to reverse this flow.

This is hard. Distraction will always have an allure because *we'll always encounter discomfort.* But "the way out is in" — the moments of discomfort that life frequently brings us are the starting point for both our distraction *and* the cure from it. If we can take these as sacred opportunities to, as Thích Nhất Hạnh urges, *look within*, we can transform our lives.

18

THE WAY OUT IS IN

I HAD BEEN SEARCHING for purpose and passion my entire adult life. It took me to investor pitch meetings and Zen monasteries, from gorgeous ruins to the heart of political movements. I wanted a life of meaning — but I kept looking around me to understand what that meaning was, albeit in more and more subtle ways.

After I got back from that first post-pandemic *sesshin*, I was hungry for more practice. I spent the summer of 2022 at Zen Mountain Monastery, working remotely and doing a couple *sesshins*. Largely outside the default world and its hungry ghost loop, I had the space I needed to begin to articulate all you've been reading — and the time to heed Thích Nhất Hạnh's words, "the way out is in."

What I remember most from that summer was the simple walk between the main monastery building and the office, where I'd hop on my laptop and do my work. The peace of those 5 minutes cut through all my narratives about my job, my angst about meaningful work, and just about everything else. Instead, I would lose my entire being in the warm sun, the distinct smell of summer in the northeast, the sound of the wind rustling the trees.

In this simple ritual, I was finding the point where purpose and meaninglessness meet. In Zen, this intersection is personified by Avalokiteshvara, the Bodhisattva or avatar of compassion. Her legend in Buddhist mythology looms large — her thousand arms are her superpower, and she uses them to pull sentient beings out of the suffering of the default world.

And yet, amidst all her compassionate labor, she's attached to nothing. Her work and her entire being are, at the heart of things, *just not that big of a deal.* As modern Zen teacher Charlotte Jojo Beck put it in one of the books from my college class, *Nothing Special*, "When we're engaged in pure activity, we're a presence, an awareness. But that's all we are. And that doesn't feel like anything. People think that the so-called enlightened state is flooded with emotional and loving feelings. But true love or compassion is simply a flow of ordinary activity."

I've come to understand Avalokiteshvara's teaching and the Bodhisattva Vow as using my whole being to live my whole life. I'm an Indian American, a bit of a product management nerd, a social justice warrior (ironically and not so ironically), an avid Zen Buddhist, and an extremely enthusiastic dude with intersectional perspectives on this mess we're all in. I can use all of that to do all I can do, not as some grand gesture but simply as a mix of the most logical and the most fun thing to do with the time between birth and death.

My Vow of Aliveness is both deeply, *personally* meaningful and simultaneously completely ordinary and pedestrian. It's not about finding the perfect project or path, but rather playing with what life is offering me *right now*, turning it into something that inspires me and, ideally, is beneficial for the people around me.

I went into that summer with the question of how I wanted to live. I came out with three truths:

- First, I contain fiery purpose. I want to do something about the problems of the default world, to be part of positive change and progress. I'm enlivened by work, relationships, and people that are *meaningful and impactful* — and if I don't prioritize these, my thirst for Aliveness turns its fire on me. There is no way for me to put my life force into something I don't care about and not respond by trying to numb out. I don't judge those who numb as a way of life — I do it myself in ways I'm still only semi-conscious of. But I know numbing, for me, results in a soul-level discontent that will inevitably take its toll on me and my loved ones.
- Second, this fiery purpose of mine needs support. The default world always stands ready to turn my purpose towards its priorities and swallow me whole. At Shopify, even after more than a decade in Zen, it was still so easy to be seduced into the numbness of corporate life. As such, my purpose needs practices and systems — pauses and regular check-ins so I know where to point it. Every time I switch on autopilot, I'm switching off my life. Designing *the way I live my life* is a process that must be continually renewed.
- And yet, third, presence is the only north star. It's the only guide I can trust, the only direction I want, the only thing I'm cultivating. All my purpose and passion, my ideas and systems, my relationships and spiritual life — they are all avenues to and servants

of the here and now. Presence is the heart of
Aliveness, and Aliveness is what I want most.

The journey of this realization brought me to the book that's
in your hands. You'll get the specifics in Part 3, but it boils
down to this: *when we know what's important, everything finds
its place.* Our priorities, the people in our lives, the passions
we want to prioritize — the puzzle pieces fit together on the
fly. Life is not too much. We're not overwhelmed. We have
exactly the time, space, and energy we need to do the things
our Aliveness is asking of us.

This is an impossible faith, and it's at the heart of our Vow. As
much as the default world is out to eat us alive, I believe that,
deep down, it's exactly what we need — steel sharpening
steel. Seeing the enormity of our task, knowing there is no
other way than forward, the Vow escapes our lips before we
even realize what it means.

ONE LAST CONFESSION: I'M STILL SCARED

Presence and Aliveness are hard, but the life of anxiety,
numbness, and unworthiness is harder. And yet, I continue to
choose the latter in so many moments. Why?

Over my many years of Zen practice, I've sat with this question, and here's my best stab at an answer: a deep-seated
terror of the vastness of my true being.

I feel this personally, every day. I am still — even now as I
write this more than 17 years into Zen training and fresh off of
a weeklong meditation retreat — terrified of the profound
silence and space that accompanies me in each moment.

Yes, I am curious about the space and silence, attracted to it,
in love with it. I am actively dedicating my life to its exploration, cultivation, and sharing.

But I am also terrified of it. I am terrified of the bottomlessness and spaciousness of my Aliveness.

Each time I set out to go to the monastery for retreat, I get nervous butterflies in my stomach — the kind I felt before a big sports game as a teenager, only larger and existential in nature. Once I get there, even as my body and mind quiet down, there is a visceral fear response that occasionally springs up. I've had countless experiences of indescribable presence and embodiment while meditating. Yet, when I feel stillness rising within me, it's sometimes met with a habitual, fearful tightening up and turning away.

At times, it feels like this terror is a constant companion, an almost holy fear, a lock on the door of my true mind. But the way out is in — the solution is within the fear, not outside of it. This terror is alive, and "alive" is where we can start. Alive is what we're after, *even when it's terrifying*. The courage needed to see this terror and to feel it — to not turn away — is the key that unlocks our authentic life.

In fact, over time, this fear has become my personal compass. Whether it's projects, relationships, places, or anything else, the more deeply something is necessary on my path of Aliveness, the more it usually carries some part of this same terror. Writing this book, for example, is something I simply have to do, and even still, I can feel a latent fear of the expansiveness, vulnerability, and beauty of this project.

One of my go-to books in moments of creative struggle is Steven Pressfield's *The War of Art*. He puts it this way: "Are you paralyzed with fear? That's a good sign. Fear is good. Like self-doubt, fear is an indicator. Fear tells us what we have to do. The more scared we are of a work [of art] or calling, the more sure we can be that we have to do it."

This fear is not calling us to transgress our boundaries, but rather asking us to dance, and to *feel*. It's asking us to show up for our lives with clear eyes and full hearts (even when they're beating a bit too fast). It's showing us the way.

The energy and practice of *vow* is the only way I know how to meet this fear in every project, relationship, and, most immediately, morning on the meditation cushion. So, as we get to the second half of our time together, I want to share what living the Vow means to me. In Part 3, I'll introduce the core framework I use for countering the default world, the Loop of Aliveness. In the last part of the book, we'll look at how this loop is brought to life in the form of rituals, practices, and communities.

PART III

THE LOOP OF ALIVENESS

Investigate impulsive consciousness.

Eihei Dogen Zenji, 13th century Zen Master

🌾

People say what we're all seeking is meaning. I don't think so. I think what we're seeking is an experience of being alive, so that our life experiences will have resonances with our own innermost being, so that we actually feel the rapture of being alive.

Joseph Campbell

🌾

Our innermost being isn't an object of its own knowledge. Just as a knife does not cut itself, fire does not burn itself, light doesn't illuminate itself, life is always an endless mystery to itself.

Alan Watts

19

A LOOPY ANTIDOTE TO THE DEFAULT WORLD

I'M SITTING at the computer with a familiar feeling right now: writer's block. I open Reddit and mindlessly scroll for a few minutes, get up for a snack, and feel the pull of a mid-morning coffee. It's one procrastination after another.

Eventually I pause, breathe, and ask myself what's going on. In response, I feel a vague restlessness and an intuitive knowing: I haven't gone outside today. So, I decide to go for a walk. I'll do my best to feel my body as it moves. I'll be with whatever body sensations or emotions arise and see what might be underneath them. And I'll almost certainly return home feeling a sense of inner connection and flow. (Update: I went rollerblading and now am, in fact, feeling less blocked. I can already feel the rest of this section flowing out of me.)

This, essentially, is the Loop of Aliveness. Loops are powerful because they visualize the momentum of our habitual behaviors and thought patterns. So far, we've seen how this momentum can work against us via seemingly small decisions and habits that lay the groundwork for our entire experience of life.

But this same dynamic can work in our favor — and the Loop of Aliveness is my model for how we do that. It both helps me understand how I'm living my life and, more importantly, gives me something I can do *right now* to cultivate Aliveness.

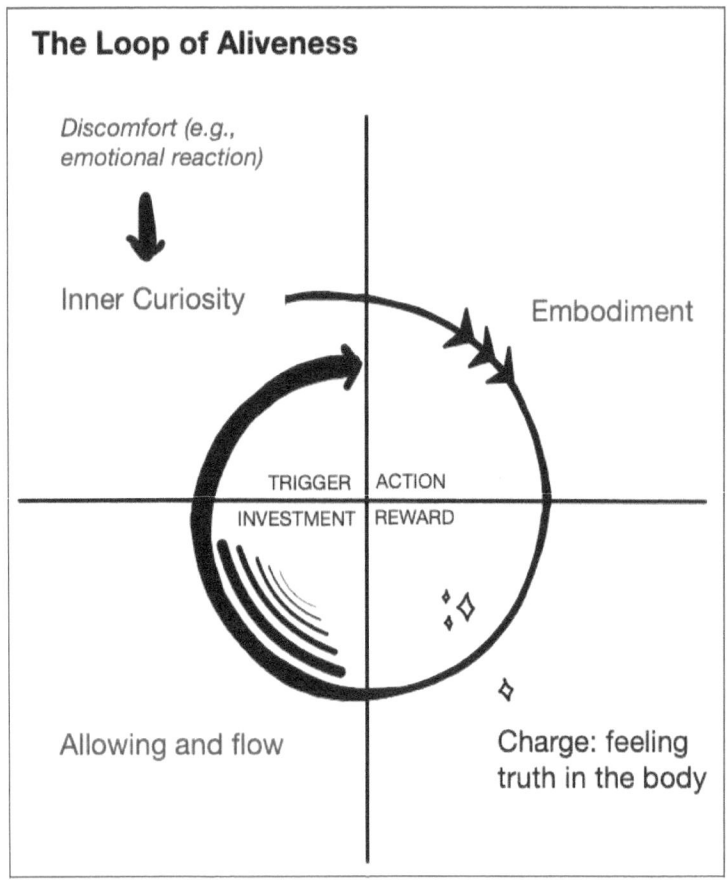

It starts off as a choice to get curious, whether in the face of discomfort, an emotional reaction we're having, or anything else. This choice is essentially an offramp to the previous loops we've looked at. In the anecdote above, it's the moment I closed Reddit and paused.

This is a radical step — it interrupts the loops of distraction, busyness, and numbness. We're practicing, choosing, and *actualizing* Aliveness over dissociation. The more energy we give the Loop of Aliveness, the weaker the force of distraction becomes and the more alive we feel.

With curiosity as a trigger, we move into embodiment — inhabiting our living, breathing bodies in the present moment. This opens the door for us to connect with and explore our feelings and the truths that live within us, which I call *charge*.

Finally, in contact with what's alive inside, we allow action to flow. We live life with more effortlessness and ease. In doing so, we find new parts of our Inner World to discover, connect with, and express in our lives — bringing us back to inner curiosity. In this way, the loop spins, and it joyfully opens up our life.

What follows is an exploration of this loop and how it functions. I'll share each step — inner curiosity, embodiment, feeling, and allowing — and how they flow together to create a dynamic relationship with our Inner World. The loop isn't meant to be a rigid formula but rather a living, breathing container for exploring and deepening our Aliveness.

With that in mind, let's take a closer look at the Loop of Aliveness. Each of its steps is an entire universe, and in cultivating any one of them, we strengthen the loop's place in our life as a whole. When we put them together, we give ourselves a path to flow between purpose and peace: discovering what's meaningful, expressing it, and enjoying the beauty and mystery of our lives as an unfolding process.

ROOTING IN PRESENCE

When I began training with my teacher, he would extol me to merge my whole identity with the experience of breathing. During one *sesshin* in 2017, he phrased this point like this: "The breath is happening right now — you only need to deal with this one breath."

Bang. Until that moment, I had carried a belief that I had to figure out my life with strategy, planning, and effort, solving my inner problems the same way I've solved my outer ones. I conceived of the journey of awakening as the arduous inner work of a lifetime, a mountain I had to climb, bit by bit. My practice was showing me the built up material of my life — the patterns, body tensions, and habits that I want to shift. Then, I was giving myself a mission: root out all my unhelpful conditioning with careful, painstaking effort.

The problem is that this method of trying to change ourselves usually involves an inner coercion that reinforces the belief that we're not good enough. We're perpetuating the trance of unworthiness.

When I heard my teacher's words, "You only need to deal with this breath," I realized that I had it backward all along. No matter how much I hated my habits of distraction, numbness, and anxiety, I wasn't going to will them out of existence. More subtly, I was never going to succeed in fixing myself if I kept *feeling* that I needed to be fixed.

My teacher was urging me to *trust presence*. It's less that "I" — (as in my ego, the sense I have of myself and my free will) — "do inner work" — and more like *inner work does me*. Insights emerge, habits shifts, stuck energy moves all on its own, and our primary task is simply to be here, open to what's alive.

YIN AND YANG

As such, the Loop of Aliveness is ultimately all about cultivating presence. There is a dance in this cultivation — a movement between *doing* and *being*. Spiritual traditions have many personifications of this dance: Shiva and Shakti in Hinduism, Isis and Osiris in Egyptian mythology, Maka and Skan amongst the Lakota, Apollo and Dionysus in ancient Greece, and countless others. However, the most popular of these is related to Zen and will be the one we use: *yang* and *yin*.

Yang is directed effort, our passions. We all have things we care about, stuff we want to give more of our time and energy towards. From art projects and hobbies to companies and social movements, we are creatures of purpose and meaning. Not only do we all deeply care about certain things, but those things *carry the Aliveness that we're seeking*. Whether the default world judges it as meaningful or useless is a distraction — it has importance *to us*, and that's all that matters.

Alongside purpose, there's an Aliveness and presence of just being, of spaciousness, of *yin*. This is *always available* to us. In Zen and countless other methods of spiritual training, we cultivate the capacity to recognize, enjoy, and live into this Aliveness with simple presence, regardless of what might be going on in our lives. We can appreciate the flowers blooming on our street whether we are grieving a loss, celebrating a win, or simply trying to get through another week at a job we don't care much for. We can receive our life, just as it is.

The Loop of Aliveness is a tool for balancing *yang* and *yin*. The primary *doing* of the loop is embodiment. The rest of the loop is, in essence, different forms of *yin* — of noticing (inner curiosity), of feeling (charge), and of flowing and non-effort (allowing). In each moment, there is a *yang* and *yin* of presence; across our lifetimes, there is a similar duality of Aliveness, moving between activity and spaciousness.

COMING INTO BALANCE

The ratio of 3 steps of *yin* to 1 of *yang* is not arbitrary — *yin* is emphasized. We live in a world out of balance — we are addicted to *yang*. Doing something seems like the only option when we're confronted with any problem or opportunity, be it relational, professional, financial, or anything else. In society at large, our economy, government, and culture are biased towards *doing* in such a fundamental way that we usually don't notice or question it.

The afflictions of the default world flow from this addiction. Patriarchy, at its root, is the global obsession of *yang* over *yin* (as is every system of oppression). Busyness, stress, and anxiety are reflections of our habitual prioritization of *doing* over *non*-doing. The lower energy counterparts to these (most notably depression) is a response to our imbalance, a desperate, exhausted movement away from *yang*.

Because of this default world bias, balance for most of us is going to lean heavily towards cultivating *yin* energy — a receptivity towards life and what it's offering us. As such, the Loop of Aliveness, for me, emphasizes this impetus towards allowing, letting go, just being. The primary thing we need to do is be present in our body. When we do this, the inner work *does* us on its own; the music of our lives dances us beautifully.

20

INNER CURIOSITY

NIGHT WAS FALLING, and I was riding my bike across the desert with a frantic edge to my pace. The year was 2014, and I was back in the magical, whimsical, and sometimes dangerous space that is Burning Man. Having gotten caught up in a fantastic conversation far from my camp, I had lost track of time. I didn't have any way to light up my body or bike, and with thousands of bikes and hundreds of large vehicles riding and driving around, I realized I could easily get hit and seriously injured.

I felt the fear rising as I set off for camp. But in my haste, I had forgotten the cape I had on. (That sentence is both ridiculous and a completely normal Burning Man thing to say.) As I turned my bike, my cape stopped flowing safely behind me and got thoroughly tangled in gears, lurching my bike to a halt.

With the sun's light dwindling, things had gotten from bad to worse. I dismounted and struggled to untangle the cape to no avail. It was getting so dark I could hardly see what I was doing. I looked around, feeling myself getting more anxious by the minute.

Then, seemingly out of nowhere, a stranger with kind eyes biked up and said, "Ahh, the cape-in-bike-gears mess. Haven't you seen The Incredibles? Capes are a bad idea." He smiled, mentioned he had plenty of lights, and asked if he could help. I was instantly set at ease. He steadily unraveled the cape, and in short order, it was fully untangled from the gears (and far less torn up than I had feared).

But my anxiety had steadily crept back up. The entire time he had been helping me out, this kind gentleman had, well, been flirting with me. He told me how great I looked and curiously asked me questions, his smile dancing with life, interest, and genuine kindness.

As we wrapped up, he invited me to stop by his camp's bar in the gayborhood later that evening. I felt myself freeze up. I gave him a stiff hug, thanked him profusely, and quickly turned to leave.

As I walked back to my bike, I wondered, "What's going on?" I was completely safe — not only was this man clearly kind and gentle, but I was bigger than him and we were in a very public space where people were always looking out for one another. My anxiety had nothing to do with any sort of safety-related concern. And yet, it was there.

As I started to mount my bike, I instinctively understood this unease was offering me an encounter with something deep within me. I let this "something deep" lead me into action. Without a second thought, I got off my bike and walked over to the man. Unfrozen, I looked him in the eyes, thanked him genuinely, and asked if I could kiss him goodbye.

Visibly stunned, he responded yes, and we kissed. Exhila-rated, he said this was one of the most incredible moments of his week. I smiled, bid him good evening, and rode off into the sunset.

I remember so vividly the euphoria — the feeling that "I'm alive!" — that took hold of me afterward. It's like a weight I had been carrying around for years just wasn't there anymore.

This isn't a coming out story. I knew before I had gotten off my bike that I wasn't gay, and I knew the same as I rode away, though the rendezvous allowed me to experience a little sliver of the vastness of attraction and connection that exist when I'm open to them.

The weight I felt being lifted was that of internalized homophobia (one of the many flavors of patriarchy, I would learn at the Undoing Patriarchy retreat two years later). With very little awareness of what was going on, I had been carrying around a set of constraining ideas about who I was and how I was supposed to be. In a single moment, I put myself in a situation where these binding cords could be cut. Now, I could feel myself elated, light as a feather.

For me, this story is a formative episode of inner curiosity — letting go of who we think we are and taking a here-and-now approach to exploring ourselves. I noticed my discomfort with his flirting, and that was my entry point. I knew immediately that something deeper was going on.

I could feel intuitively that I was putting myself in a sort of box. I was curious about what might happen if — for just one relatively safe moment — I allowed myself to be someone *outside* that box. It ended up opening up my heart in a profound way.

STARTING THE LOOP

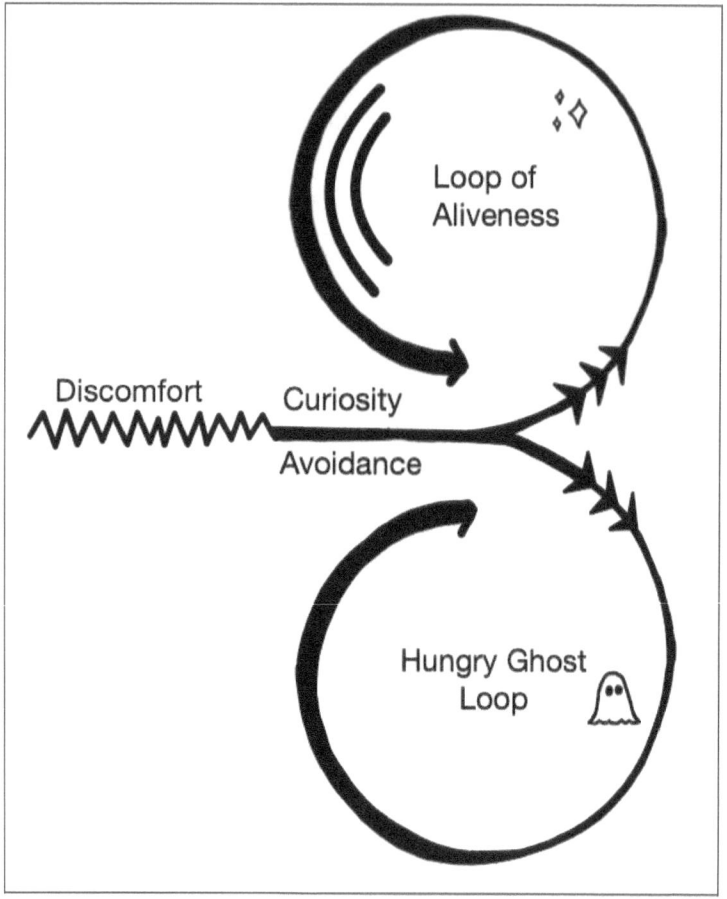

Inner curiosity does not always express itself in such a dramatic dropping away of internalized homophobia. But when we find ourselves feeling uncomfortable (consciously or otherwise), we're being offered a sacred choice: curiosity or avoidance, Aliveness or the life of a hungry ghost.

We make this choice a thousand times a day, as discomfort finds us in its infinite forms: the discomfort of experiencing something we don't want to be experiencing, not having something we want, physical pain, emotional distress, spiritual listlessness, and countless others. The momentum of these choices essentially dictates the quality of our lives. Deciding to look under the surface is our gateway out of our habitual, distracted ways of life and the beginning of a more dynamic relationship with our Inner World.

Inner curiosity starts with the simple thought, "I wonder what's really going on here." It's an attitude of being more inquisitive and less sure of what we think is happening inside us and even who we think we are. It requires courage and openness — in the example of meeting this man at Burning Man, I had to be willing to not simply bolt (which I was so close to doing!) and instead look at my discomfort as a starting point of an exploration.

But the most challenging part about inner curiosity is that it's, say, 95% non-intellectual. When we hear Master Dogen's exhortation to "investigate impulsive consciousness," we might think about *a-ha* moments in therapy, journaling, or in a conversation with a friend.

These insights help us understand why we are the way we are, but they're only about 5% of what inner curiosity is about. In my Burning Man example, I now have a nice, tidy story to tell you about internalized homophobia. But in the moment, I was just *there*, moving through a live, in-my-face encounter and making a snap decision to trust and follow a hunch about how I wanted to respond. Reasoning and understanding intellectually can get in the way of letting presence lead.

Practiced in this way, inner curiosity has the power to take any situation in which discomfort is arising and turn it around, using it as fuel for going inward. In time, we start to reorient to discomfort as a sign to go deeper, rather than something to run from. When we feel a pull to pick up our phone in a quiet moment of waiting, we might just pause and ask ourselves, "What's going on? What am I avoiding or not feeling in this moment?" And rather than try to answer that question with another thought, we sit in silence and feel what arises. We move our attention into our bodies.

21

EMBODIMENT

THE WARM SUNDAY morning light peaks through the huge stained glass windows that adorn the walls of the church that I'm in. My eyes come to rest on the vast open space in front of me. There is no preacher, no pews of seated congregants. I'm not here for a religious gathering — although, maybe I am.

People are all around me. Most are dancing to the music offered by a DJ on a small stage, while some are stretching or meditating along the walls. Each person's movement is their own. Some are on the beat, others waving around at their own pace, still others shaking their bodies as if they were trying to get dry. There are probably 200 humans present, and yet no one is conversing.

I discovered this gathering, called ecstatic dance, in 2021. Its rules are simple: it's a practice of moving and grooving (or if it feels right, *not* moving and grooving) without conversation or intoxication. The scene is visually and aurally similar to a nightclub, but the point is simply to be — to move and express without judgment or fear of it.

Dances were (and still are) held outdoors or in the big indoor space I described, the Church of 8 Wheels in the Lower Haight neighborhood of SF. Between the open space and masking, they felt safe enough to attend, and they quickly became the perfect antidote to my tech worker life. Ecstatic dance was everything I was craving: flow, connection, and an opportunity to inhabit my body in movement.

It is, in many ways, a strange place. There are no prescribed norms of behavior to guide what to do or how to move. It's you, your body, and the music — and perhaps the invitation to let the walls between these three come down.

For me, the core of ecstatic dance is a practice of being in my body, feeling whatever arises, and allowing whatever movement that wants to happen. On these Sunday mornings, I have found myself cackling with laughter, shouting with joy, and shaking my body while tears roll down my face — sometimes all at the same time!

It stands in such stark relief to the rest of my life. There is nothing to gain, no status to be had, no specific thing I must do, nor is it much of an opportunity to meet other people.

Sometimes, I notice default world mind states poke through. I worry about what other people might think of my dancing and feel self-conscious about how I look and move. I deliberate about how to get the most out of my time: the most healing, the most expression, the most play — anything that I can maximize.

But that's the exact opposite of what I'm there to do. When I notice I'm lost in these kinds of thoughts, I come back. In this way, ecstatic dance is a core practice of embodiment — of bringing my awareness into my direct physical experience and letting my body move and express itself. It can be painful, constricted, flowing, joyful, connective, and enlivening — all within the space of a couple hours.

COMING HOME TO THE BODY

Embodiment is the place that I channel my *doing* energy. More than thinking, reading books, or anything else, *embodiment* is the most fundamental activity of Aliveness, the "action" step of the loop. Taking a breath, feeling our feet on the floor, hearing the sounds around us, touching someone (consensually) — it can take a variety of forms and is always available. There is no place that's not appropriate for embodiment: at my desk writing these words, waiting for the stoplight to change at an intersection, in the midst of a frenzied schedule or a difficult conversation with a loved one.

Embodiment is sacred because *our Inner World exists within our very body.* By coming into direct contact with it, we create the conditions for Inner World connection. In an almost mystical way, embodiment is the knife that cuts away our conditioning and reveals to us our inner wisdom. It is no accident that nearly every system of meditation or yoga begins with an embodied practice, whether it's breath meditation in Zen and other forms of Buddhism, movement practice in yoga, or others.

Embodiment is not always easy. The more we feel our bodies, the more we feel our pain. This realization has, at times, been one of the hardest parts of my own journey into presence. During ecstatic dance, for example, I notice that certain parts of my body feel deeply uncomfortable. They've been clenched and numb for so long that when I become aware of them, there's a lot of pain present.

But over time, what I've learned is that the hard part is more the *fear* of the pain rather than the experience of it. Because when I stay with my body, it's not that I'm just feeling more pain — it's that I'm feeling more *body*. There is so much sensation coming from my physical being, and so often, this sensation is joy, pleasure, and wonder. The more I let myself just experience moments of pain directly, the more they're simply a human body sensation to be experienced, alongside a universe of other human body sensations. (Note: the type of pain I experience is usually not excruciating or tied to a medical condition. For some, this orientation toward feeling pain may not be supportive.)

The opposite is also true. When we choose numbness to avoid pain, we actually increase our pain (often at a subconscious level) because our bodies stay clenched *and* we reinforce our fear of our aching. Over time, our mind comes to the (usually subconscious) belief that our body is too painful to feel, and we lock in forms of dissociation as simply how we live. On top of this, by vacating our bodies, we dull our ability to feel pleasure, taking us farther away from our inherent Aliveness.

The energy of our negative emotions and sensations gets stored in our bodies, usually in the form of chronic tension or clenching in our muscles. We then organize our patterns of thought, behavior, and emotion around avoiding feeling our tightness (usually subconsciously). In our constriction, we feel less alive *as a baseline experience of life.*

THE BODY KEEPS THE SCORE

The core problem is that, at some level within us, we're *choosing* the discomfort of anxious thoughts as the best option for ourselves. Our internal belief is that these are more bearable and less threatening and painful than being present to the body.

The only way out of this conundrum is embodiment. In practicing it, we grow our ability to more directly feel our bodies and the universe of sensations they present us (even if they're painful). We're essentially saying no to numbness — and wildly saying yes to simply resting our attention in the body sensations we're experiencing *right now*.

Dr. Bessel van der Kolk goes into this process at length in his bestselling book, *The Body Keeps The Score*: "Being frightened means that you live in a body that is always on guard. Angry people live in angry bodies. In order to change, people need to become aware of their sensations and the way that their bodies interact with the world around them."

For me, embodiment is a fundamental practice that I take up in a variety of ways. Stretching, yoga, dance, working out, walking, singing, and even eating can help us move our awareness into our body. In the realm of therapy, "somatic experiencing" has become quite popular for its embodied focus. Meditation is my most fundamental body practice, a chance to experience stillness within my physical being. I'll go deeper into these types of practices in the next chapters.

Embodiment looks different for each of us. It intersects with health and physical ability in a myriad of ways. Chronic conditions and disabilities can make embodiment practices more complex. My wish is for folks to discover embodiment in whatever ways possible, but also that this does not increase suffering nor reinforce the trance of unworthiness in any way.

However we do it, in the context of the Loop of Aliveness, practicing embodiment is crucial because it cultivates our capacity for getting out of our heads. Over time, the body becomes our north star, and this tangibly brings us more deeply into life.

22

CHARGE

IN LATE SEPTEMBER 2023, I hosted a series of workshops around using the Loop of Aliveness to guide goal- and aspiration-setting. These workshops were a revelation. It was deeply inspiring to see people articulate dreams and intentions that they didn't know were there and then figure out how to turn their visions into reality — all in the space of a couple hours.

After leading the last workshop, I took a walk through nearby Buena Vista Park in San Francisco to decompress. My body was buzzing, and soon I began to notice an energy more powerful and directed than most feelings I usually encounter: I needed to keep exploring the terrain of this workshop. I wanted to write it all out. Everything. What makes me so passionate about connecting to our Inner World, why it's so hard, and how certain frameworks and practices can help us infuse what's meaningful into our everyday lives.

My whole body was palpably resonating with this notion, a feeling of joyful electricity running through my limbs and spine. There was a bounce in my step, a lightness in my arms and whole being. By the time I got back to my apartment, I was clear — *I needed to write this book.*

Realizations like this are special because they're rooted in *charge*. Charge is a word I use to describe *the felt energy of our personal truths.* It's everything from the subtle confidence of intuition to the root, core, deep down *oomph* underneath all the inspired action we take. Feeling charge means we're coming into contact with an opening, a channel connecting the depths of the Inner World with our mind, body, and/or heart.

Charge takes infinite forms. For me, it's frequently electrical, energetic, and embodied — a burst of an inner emotional energy. For example, when my whole body lights up when I meet someone, I might instinctively feel they're going to be an important person in my life.

THE SOMETIMES TERRIFYING POWER OF CHARGE

It was the last full day of *sesshin* in October 2019 at ZMM. We had just finished the afternoon block of meditation, and I desperately needed everyone to leave the meditation hall.

For three straight hours, I had felt an enormous emotional energy inside of me, concentrated in my neck. And for three hours, I just felt it. Each time my meditative attention floated away, I would gently bring it back to the energy, to the sensations in my lower neck.

I was just feeling, feeling, feeling — staying grounded in my breath and the cushion beneath me. And during the last period, something exploded inside of me.

I managed to mostly keep it together during the short chanting that followed the last sitting period. A millisecond after the last person left the *zendo*, the floodgates erupted. For about half an hour, I ugly cried as hard as I ever have, a vague feeling of deep fear washing over me.

And I had no idea why. Eventually, I was able to gather myself and go outside, skipping dinner as I was, very clearly, in no state to eat. As I walked, the intensity abided, and I started to wonder: What in the world was going on? Where was this coming from?

All I could sense was an amorphous dread. Slowly, a memory came to me: an out-of-body experience I'd had more than five years ago.

In 2013, on the recommendation of a friend, I did a float in a sensory deprivation tank. Float tanks, as they're called, are body-sized pods filled with skin-temperature water. The water is so salty that one can float without effort. The closed pod hatch makes it completely dark, and they're usually kept quite silent. As such, they're a particularly unique type of meditation because there is almost zero sensory stimulation and the body is so effortlessly supported by the water, allowing for deep relaxation.

And in this relaxation, towards the end of the float, I noticed that my sense of "I" was below my body. My body was a corpse, hovering peacefully above what felt like *me*.

There was a profound sense of peace and wonder, but this only lasted a second before terror kicked in. Hard. It was one of the most exhilarating experiences of my life, but I was also shaken to my core. Afterward, I felt my neck tighten, and this tightness had remained in some form ever since. Now, for the first time in what felt like forever, my neck felt light and unencumbered.

This is a seminal story for me when it comes to charge. Here's what happened: As I was steadily practicing inner curiosity and embodiment while meditating in the space and silence of *sesshin*, I eventually encountered a depth of emotion and feeling that I had been avoiding for years. The clenching I'd felt for so long had been fear lodged as a clinging stuckness in my neck. This was centered on the place where my consciousness and sense of self had escaped away during that float. The actual depth of my terror and sadness of that moment was kept away from my conscious mind.

Feeling this depth was an experience full of charge — and it freed my body (and mind) into lightness and deeper Aliveness.

TRAUMA, PROCESSING, AND BEYOND

As we live more embodied, we encounter the charge that lives in the depths of our Inner World and the liberation it is offering us. Sometimes, that's inspiration in the form of a drive to write this book. In other moments, it will include tougher stuff, like this explosion of embodied emotion while on *sesshin*.

The "tougher stuff" is often our trauma, though this can be a hard word to define. For our purposes, it's any inner or outer event that we don't feel fully in the moment or that causes us to dissociate in some way. This creates an unfelt energetic residue inside of us. The residue results in a tightening or closing of our bodies or hearts, and we often adopt habits, postures, and thought patterns to numb the pain from this clenching.

As we come into contact with this residue, our attention metabolizes our pain, and it runs through our system. This phenomenon is often called processing, and it's what happened when I encountered the tightness, pain, and sadness in my neck on retreat. Feeling that pain was a profoundly healing experience, even if it was uncomfortable in the moment.

But we need to be careful to not let the concept of "processing" turn into yet another way we disconnect from ourselves. We can so easily categorize uncomfortable emotions and body sensations as bad things that we need to get rid of. When we try to "process" our feelings from this place, it reduces our relationship with our Inner World into utility and minimization rather than love and curiosity. Our feelings want to be *felt* — intimately, lovingly, fully — not "processed" as quickly as possible like a product on a conveyor belt.

As such, what's most important in the Loop of Aliveness is that we receive the moments of charge of our Inner World with presence, respect, and openness. As hard as it can be, we're staying receptive rather than trying to fix how we're feeling. The point is to fall in love with feeling for its own sake. This is at first an uncomfortable leap of faith, but slowly, over time, it turns into the reality that our lives are much richer, fuller, and less painful if we feel fully instead of turning away.

CHARGE, PRESENT AND LASTING

The unique thing about charge is that it's both instantaneous and an energy that can stick around. From relationships and work projects to flowers on my block and everyday views of my beloved San Francisco, I've found that the critical, lasting, meaningful things in my life have a corresponding charge in my Inner World. That is, when I'm present with these things, they produce an inner energetic sensation of meaning that seems to last.

The writing of this book, for example, is consistently powered by the present-moment version of that first charge that I felt a year ago. The charge has changed, as have I, but it's still moving me to write this book. In this way, charge lets us tune into what has meaning, what *actually* is bringing us to life right now.

But charge guides us, not the other way around. We cannot control charge or our experience of it. It's entirely possible that I will wake up tomorrow and the charge to write this book will be gone. If that happens, I probably have to stop writing, or risk creating something contrived.

This is, to be sure, a *scary* process. Charge can be nourished, but it can't be manufactured. I can't think or reason my way into feeling it. If I want to root my life in truth, I need to be open to my truth changing. As much as I might want to finish a book (or keep working on a company or stay in a romantic relationship), if my effort is *not* being powered by charge, it's going to be part of "the life others expect of me" in one way or another.

Again, this is frightening. From the conventional point of view, trusting charge offers us far less control over our lives. But that control was actually a mirage — it took our stress, anxiety, and inauthenticity to hold in place. In fact, trusting charge is only scary because we're so accustomed to our own inauthenticity as a way of life.

Fortunately, like anything we're accustomed to, our reliance on artificial charge can be shifted. Our truth draws life from the present, and the more we dwell in Aliveness, the stronger our trust in charge becomes.

Charge is the mysterious reward within the Loop of Aliveness. It's both a felt sense of meaning *and* a trailhead for deeper exploration. It's the inspiration for writing this book *and* the energy that powers the writing. It's the repressed emotional energy of trauma in my neck, the power it expresses when I'm open to consciously receiving it, *and* the moment of experiencing and healing as I come into contact with it.

At its best, the truth within our charge powers us through and past the blocks of our minds. It clarifies, cures, and, at times, moves into action. There are infinite flavors of charge — it can be big and small, positive or negative. Really, all we need to do is be present and notice charge. Over time, we learn how to understand it, work with it — and allow our truth to lead our life.

23

ALLOWING

I'M WRITING this on a bright, clear morning in San Francisco. We've had a bunch of rain recently, and the blue skies are inviting me out for a walk. I'm already contemplating lunch, and whether I'll combine a stroll with a food stop or make lunch at home before heading out for a bit.

How would you handle this situation? For me, if I'm not intentional about it, I'll be kicking it around all morning in some corner of my brain. I'll look at lunch places' menus in moments of procrastination, think about the food I have in the fridge, and probably fret that any place I go would be at least $15. (I blame inflation, not San Francisco. SF already gets enough unwarranted grief.) It would be like a small thorn in my mind, keeping me from being present and introducing an element of inner drama that, annoyingly, part of me seems to enjoy.

It's such a habit pattern that I wouldn't think twice about it. I might not even notice its impact on my work or imagine that there would be an entirely different way to navigate these sorts of situations.

But instead, in these moments, I rely on the Loop of Aliveness. Staying present and embodied (rather than getting lost in the mental deliberation), I ask myself what I want to do for lunch. And then, just for a few seconds, I breathe, sit back, and wait. I turn my sense of listening around and focus on my body and allow for an answer to emerge. In this situation, it was quite clear: I'm feeling like getting a sandwich from a new place down the road.

In the next few moments, I notice the desire to take this new development and feed it back into the thought machine — am I picking the right place? Am I sure I don't want to go to my usual spot, where I know what I'll get? Shouldn't I just save the money and eat at home?

What happens next is a crucial choice. If I take that answer I received when I quieted down and listened to myself and run it through more evaluating and back-and-forth thinking — and maybe even change it to something else — what sort of message does that send to my Inner World? Putting ourselves in the shoes of our Inner World, how would you feel if a loved one asked you to express your desire and then turned it around and questioned it?

Obviously, we need to check intuition with reason, but for something so simple and unimportant in the grand scheme of things, this is a moment to trust and not overthink. Our habit of overthinking is exactly what disrupts the trust we're building with our Inner World — and it's often driven by a self-critiquing energy rooted in the trance of unworthiness.

Allowing means to let our lives flow. By accepting my lunchtime answer without too much deliberation, I'm not just deepening inner trust, but I'm choosing my Vow. As my friend Melissa said in a recent conversation, , "the Vow is the big picture, the direction, the priority to which everything in life is put up against." Picking the perfect place for lunch (which isn't even possible in the first place!) pales in comparison.

PEACEFUL FLOW

When I think about allowing and the peace it cultivates, my incredible backpacking trip is the first thing that comes to mind. It's an odd association, as the trip was full of activity — some of the wildest and most interesting activity of my life. And yet, from the chaotic streets of Cairo to villages and trails in the Himalayas, the abiding feeling of the trip was that of peace.

Why was the trip so peaceful? It wasn't because I was free from the constraints of a job or working life. It wasn't that I was by myself for such an extended period of time. It wasn't even the breathtaking natural scenery that accompanied me for so much of my travels, though these all certainly helped.

As best as I can tell, it was because once I set out, I mostly let go of the reins and allowed my Inner World to lead. I had some idea of an itinerary, but in the day-to-day, I wasn't trying to wrangle my experience in one direction or another. If I was delayed in the freezing Moscow airport for 24 hours or riding an 18-hour bus through central India, so be it. That's just where I was.

I was noticing what brought me to life and allowing myself to flow in that direction. It cultivated an undeniable sense that, in each moment, *I'm in the exact place I need to be.* Without having anything figured out, my life, exactly as it is, is perfectly ok.

Really, "I'm in the exact place I need to be" dramatically undersells what I'm talking about here. On that trip, there were more than two dozen 12-24 hour travel adventures: buses through rural Turkey or around the Sinai peninsula, train trips across Egypt and India, a shared taxi over the Rohtang Pass, and many more. As far as I can remember, *I was rarely, if ever, bored.* Or irritated, or annoyed. It seems almost unimaginable to my 38-year-old self sitting and writing this book in my San Francisco apartment. If I didn't have the journal to prove it on my bookshelf, I wouldn't even believe it myself.

That, I believe, is the power of flow. Conventionally, we might think this sort of equanimity arises from patience. Instead, I feel like patience is more the effect than the cause, the natural result of being in trust and alignment with our Inner World.

This alignment does not require a blissful, once-in-a-lifetime trip, though. A year ago, I was navigating a painful breakup. For about a month, I would wake up every night at 3am with a mix of grief and anxiety. Once this pattern became clear, I developed a routine: I'd take a short walk around the block, light a candle, and begin my morning meditation. Sometimes, I'd get sleepy after an hour or two, and I'd return to bed. On other days, I'd sit, and when I felt complete, I'd start my day. While I was annoyed and occasionally bemoaned the situation, I mostly embraced it.

The 3am wake ups dissolved in a few weeks. It was another episode of the power of allowing. Whatever happens, *yes this mess, yes this magic, yes this life.*

Allowing does not mean there aren't times when we need to draw boundaries, raise our voices, and even get angry. But so often, these can come from a place of reactivity, from our impulsive consciousness. Instead, in this step of the Loop of Aliveness, we're letting our Inner World guide us, *responding* from a centered, curious place rather than reacting hastily.

Allowing holds and supports the entire Loop. In a sense, it offers less control than the usual way of managing our lives with our thoughts and actions. But in its place, we receive an enormous gift — the gift of simplicity, of peace of mind, of trusting relationship with our Inner World.

24

STAYING IN THE LOOP
THROUGH PAIN AND PLEASURE

I DID a double-take when I saw his age on the roster. He was only 26, the youngest patient I had seen in the Intensive Care Unit (ICU). I was at the Kaiser Hospital in Oakland, where I volunteer as a Buddhist/interfaith chaplain every other week. For a couple hours, I visit each room on the 6th floor and see if the patient there wants to chat about what's up for them, whether it's emotionally, spiritually, or anything else.

Feeling concerned that someone so young had ended up here, I took a deep breath, knocked on the door, and walked in. "Hi Eduardo, my name is Ravi and I'm a volunteer chaplain with the spiritual care department. How's it going?"

Eduardo shared that he had landed in the ICU after his most recent bout with alcohol addiction and the wreckage it had caused in his life. He was palpably uncomfortable in his bed, constantly fidgeting while speaking. I asked if he wanted to spend a few moments simply breathing, and he agreed it might help. I guided him through a short meditation. Slowly, his body began to relax.

He told me his story, recounting in detail what alcohol had done to him: the loved ones he abandoned, the jobs lost, the damage to his body, inside and out. He was quite present, feeling the impact of his story as he shared it.

Eventually, the conversation turned to what came next, and, within only a question or two of my asking, he started to talk about how he was going to get better. He had a plan, he was strong, and he knew he could do this. Over the 30 minutes we spent together, I saw him connect with his body and, from that connection, draw on a confidence and strength that seemed to naturally emerge.

It was a beautiful example of what can happen when pain is met with presence. Our lives are filled with pain, and these so often cause us to exit the Loop of Aliveness. So far, we've focused on the ordinary discomforts of everyday life, but there's also the deeper stuff: injuries, sickness, losses of loved ones via death or parting, and more.

I believe these are sacred opportunities. Meeting these seasons of our life with presence is one of the most profoundly life-giving choices we can make. When I'm hit with a rough stretch, the Loop short-circuits my confusion and simplifies my world. Curiosity, embodiment, charge, allowing — where can I lean in? I don't need to stress, I just need to find my entry point.

In *Letters to a Young Poet*, Rainer Maria Rilke writes:

"So don't be frightened, dear friend, if a sadness confronts you larger than any you have ever known, casting its shadow over all you do. You must think that something is transforming within you, and remember that life has not forgotten you; it holds you in its hand and will not let you fall. Why would you want to exclude from your life any uneasiness, any pain, any depression, since you don't know what work they are accomplishing within you?"

This is incredibly hard. In the face of death, the end of relationships, or crises of any sort, the urge to dissociate and distract ourselves can be overwhelming. At times, we may even *need* this — distractions can be used mindfully, giving us space to gather ourselves.

But then we must come back and find a way to move through our breakdowns with presence. When difficult times are upon us, we have the potential to encounter our deepest truths, to traverse the most remote crevices of our Inner World and bring back new light that illuminates our way forward.

Meeting the hard stuff with presence is challenging, and fortunately, there's a flip side: pleasure.

THE LIFE-CHANGING MAGIC OF PLEASURE

In the Winter of 2015, I found myself in a lavender field. More specifically, in a small lavender farm and brewery at a hostel in El Bolson, a backpacker town nestled in the northern part of Argentinian Patagonia. I was escaping the New York winter there, working remotely for Avaaz.org and enjoying the sunshine and nature.

The hostel had lavender everywhere. As potpourri scattered around the buildings and grounds in small bowls. Baked into homemade sweets. Essenced into soaps. Even their website has a lavender color scheme. Walking through the garden surrounded by lavender was an ecstatic sensory explosion.

And I stumbled upon a major realization during that trip, one that would have earth-shattering ramifications for my life.

I, uh, liked lavender.

The smell. The color. Even the taste.

How had I not known this before? Maybe it was a gender thing — I didn't even realize that, as a man, I *could* like lavender. Zooming out, it was deeply linked to how I deprioritized *pleasure*. Each form of lavender was simple, soft, and luxurious — and before that trip, my conditioning just wouldn't let me access the pleasure these gave me.

I laugh thinking about it now, but at the time, it was truly mind-blowing. Where had this been my whole life? (Or more accurately, where had *I* been?)

When I got back home to Brooklyn, I bought some lavender-colored sheets and lavender essential oil and even made lavender candles. I was shocked at how many small moments of joy they brought me. Lavender has stuck around — as I write this, I'm getting a whiff of the lavender incense burning across the room.

The story might seem a bit ridiculous to you; telling it feels a bit silly for me. But it's an essential one. Pleasure is an incredible way to invite ourselves into Aliveness.

What is pleasure? The smell of a lavender field. A sip of coffee nestled up with a book. A specific chord in a song. The feeling of the sun on my skin. The last rays of light on the amber hills around San Francisco. A hand in mine. (These are a few of my favorite things.)

Pleasure is anything that *feels good*. It's not really rooted in thought, but it can include mental activity. It is the giving of our attention to the embodied sensation of pleasure — the taste, sound, touch, sight, and smell of it. It's simple, direct, and in the moment. It's fundamentally *easeful*.

And it's absolutely crucial in the Loop of Aliveness. In their book *Pleasure Activism,* adrienne maree brown writes, "Pleasure is the point. Feeling good is not frivolous, it is freedom. It is not one of the spoils of capitalism. It is what our bodies, our human systems, are structured for; it is the aliveness and awakening, the gratitude and humility, the joy and celebration of being miraculous."

Pleasure — and our non-anxious receiving of it — sets not just our nervous systems but our whole lives at ease. It makes our bodies a favorable place to call home. It calms our mind and feeds our heart and soul. Doing things for pleasure and then enjoying that pleasure (and letting go of grasping for more of it) is a fundamental practice of Aliveness.

THE DIFFICULTIES OF PLEASURE

Pleasure can be a complicated experience for a few reasons. First and foremost, we can't be assured of it. We can do something we think we like, but as we move into the activity, it might not actually feel pleasurable in the moment. A massage can hurt more than it feels good, for example. We carry expectations of satisfaction into a pleasurable activity, and when these aren't met, we can end up judging the experience, others, or even ourselves.

Second, within capitalism, we're quick to commoditize pleasure as an act of consumption, rather than experience it from a state of presence. This commoditization fuels the cycle of attachment and clinging — we long for the next hit without really feeling the pleasure we're experiencing right now.

Similarly, we might not believe we deserve pleasure. The default world has fed us so many messages about which types of bodies can feel good in which ways. Caught in the trance of unworthiness, we may feel we need to suffer in some way to earn the right to delight and satisfaction — or that we're not deserving of it in the first place.

Fourth, from a psychological perspective, most of us have a negativity bias. According to Wikipedia, negativity bias means that "something very positive will generally have less of an impact on a person's behavior and cognition than something equally emotional but negative." We tend to notice, fixate on, and identify with pain more than pleasure. In a really straightforward way, negativity gives us a lot more material. When we get together with friends, we can spend a lot of time talking about the bad or hard stuff. When it comes to the good stuff, there often isn't that much to say! In a really basic way, it's easy to *forget* pleasure.

Finally, we're usually moving too quickly, not noticing when our Inner World is telling us what it likes. The joy of lavender was too subtle for me to notice until I was literally immersed in a field of it. Pleasure is a great motivator for training our attention (it certainly was for me in my first few years of practice).

Each of these blockers to pleasure is surmountable with practice, and pleasure comes in many forms. Some are more active and movement-oriented, like exercise and hikes; others involve slowness and rest, like restorative yoga practices, lavender, or a spa day. Another dimension of pleasure is play and creativity. Creating something simple — taking time to artfully plate a meal, making a playlist we love, even drawing or doodling for the fun of it — is a fantastic way to inject pleasure into our lives.

25

THE LOOP AND SOCIAL IDENTITY

"HI, I'M RAVI." It's an innocuous line, something I've uttered thousands of times. And yet, when I said it in a bar one chilly evening during my first winter in New York City, I finally *heard* the words coming out of my mouth.

I was saying my name wrong. And I had been doing it for as long as I could remember.

Specifically, I was mispronouncing the "a," saying my name "rah-vee" (as if the "a" rhymed with the "o" in "copy"). In actuality, my name is pronounced "ruh-vee," as if it rhymes with "love-y."

How long had I been doing this? My memory was foggy, but somewhere in my childhood, I stopped saying my own name right. I wanted to fit in, and every non-Indian person I met called me "rah-vee," so that became my name.

I started to introduce myself correctly ("ruh-vee"), and I noticed a funny thing — I would say "ruh-vee," and the person would respond, "Hi, rah-vee." (To this day, I don't know why this happens. I think we have a subconscious mental process where we turn sounds into letters, and letters back into sound in the moments between hearing "Hi, I'm ruh-vee" and replying, "Hi, rah-vee.")

Once in a while, though, whether because they were Indian or simply a keen listener, someone would say my name correctly upon meeting me ("hi, ruh-vee"). The surge of intimacy — feeling *seen* — was instant. It was the name my parents called me, that so many beloved family members and friends used for me during the vulnerable and magical years of childhood.

It was time for a long-overdue change. I pulled together a list of close friends who had been saying my name wrong and sent them an email. I assured them it wasn't their fault, but that I'd appreciate it if they started saying my name correctly (and totally understood if it took them a while to adjust). I can happily report that now, the dear ones in my life pronounce my name correctly — and the intimacy and gratitude I feel have not dampened since I first made this change more than a decade ago. Over the years of practicing meditation, I've realized the impact of this isn't just psychological. I feel the shift in closeness and intimacy with others in my body.

SOCIAL IDENTITY AND THE DEFAULT WORLD

In a small but simple way, my habit of mispronouncing my name was blocking me from a set of feelings in my body — from *embodiment*. The charge of love and closeness I'd feel with someone was diminished when they said my name wrong. This made it harder to simply *allow*, to flow in relationships and trust the connection. As the important people in my life began pronouncing my name correctly, I felt my heart open up and my trust in them grow from this simple change.

There is a whole world here — emotions we bypass due to our habit patterns around social identity. This terrain has unfortunately become a hot-button topic, but I want to start with a simple truth: *different bodies have different experiences of society, culture, and relationship.* The default world conditions us based in part on our social identity — our body type, race, class, gender, sexual orientation, and so on. Because Aliveness is unlocked by unraveling this conditioning, there are parts of our journey that will need to specifically look at the relationship between the markers of our identity and the workings of our mind and heart.

There's a lot of big stuff here — vast inequities across lines of race, gender, etc. that have a significant impact on the material realities of our lives. However, in my experience, it's the little things that have been truly eye-opening. For example, in a situation in which I'm meeting new people (and no one knows each other previously), if I'm in a conversation with two white people, they'll look at each other more than they'll look at me. As I noticed this over and over, I got curious and used these moments as a chance to embody. I felt a sense of unimportance, unworthiness, and even shame — emotions that I had been unaware of. My normal reaction in many of these situations was to talk more and take up space — I realized this was a knee-jerk reaction stemming my desire to be seen and feel valued.

I began to realize just how deeply these experiences were embedded across my life. Growing up in a world in which whiteness was synonymous with inclusion, normalcy, and even beauty meant that I frequently felt like an outsider. For years, I was driven by a desire to date white people as a way of feeling a sense of value and inclusion. As I've shed conditioning around this, I've found myself authentically attracted to a much broader range of people. It's been wild to see how much of something I thought was so intrinsic — attraction — was actually rooted in conditioning.

Though we may or may not notice, the default world's biases are always being communicated to us. And our mental and relational patterns form as a reaction to this — to help us preserve a sense of worthiness, secure resources, avoid guilt, and so on. This reaction blocks our embodiment and even our curiosity — exploring how we're really feeling can result in big emotions, one that can be disruptive to our relationships and even our social standing.

I want to share my take on the core dynamics of this process as it relates to Aliveness. Because this is not a book about social identity, I'll have to generalize in a way that may rub the wrong way or simply not ring true. I ask your forgiveness — I felt this material was too important to ignore because it has been so impactful for me in my journey of coming *alive*. As always, take what makes sense and leave the rest.

THE DEFAULT REPRESSION WITHIN SOCIAL IDENTITY

In short, almost all of us have repressed, unfelt emotions in the realm of social identity and our experiences within it. Our default world conditioning is consistently reducing us, pushing us away from our full humanity — whether we've been the recipients of privilege or the victims of bias and injustice. (And all of us have elements of both.)

To the extent we have a non-dominant social identity, we're probably carrying around unconscious rage. The state of the world rightly makes us angry, but to feel this anger — to even acknowledge its existence — is extraordinarily unsafe. Starting with pronouncing my name correctly, I went down the racial rabbit holes of my Inner World. As I dug up the emotional remnants of a lifetime of marginalization (almost all small-scale, to be clear), I would encounter red-hot charges of fury and pain.

Exploring this was hard. If I didn't have dear ones in my life who could forgive the rants I sometimes went on, I probably would have lost many friends. Fortunately, over time, my commitment to embodiment has metabolized much of this anger. Now, it's mostly a passenger, friend, and even a purveyor of Aliveness. The rage is there, and it's *okay*. This *okayness* has opened up space for curiosity, embodiment, and the charge of energy and empathy that I now have access to in my everyday life.

Similarly, as I began to understand during the Undoing Patriarchy retreat, so many of my habitual responses in the realm of gender were rooted in guilt. It came up in the smallest, most innocent of ways. I'd get uncomfortable when a female friend or romantic partner talked about menstrual cramps and the pain of being on their period. I'd quickly suggest ways to try to make it better. I had a hard time *just hearing* their experience and letting it be. I had a basic discomfort with the simple fact that their body had a whole arena of pain and suffering that I was magically free from. Again, I constructed entire habit patterns to avoid the discomfort of guilt.

There are countless dynamics like these — emotions, reactions, and truths about the world that we're subconsciously and behaviorally laboring to ignore. We may even know this, at some level. In a viral classroom clip, American educator Janet Elliot asked a classroom of a hundred or so white students: "I want to do an experiment: every white person in this room, who would be happy to be treated as this society in general treats our Black citizens, please stand."

Crickets. Nobody stood up. She repeated herself, and the room stayed silent and motionless. My guess is the majority of students in that room knew that they would not want to trade places with Black folks, but to have it be pointed out so directly was likely jarring.

This is normal. We reflexively turn away from uncomfortable truths like this one (especially if we have the social identity/privilege to do so). It's deeply uncomfortable. And yet just like every instance of this dynamic we've looked at, our turning away from discomfort chips away at our Aliveness.

FROM REPRESSION TO ALIVENESS

I believe that, regardless of our specific social identity, our repression has a common root: heartache and unworthiness. Staying with both guilt and anger, for me, has led to an underlying grief over our default world and systems that marginalize so many. Even being privileged is ultimately a sad situation — we're valued for some superficial aspect of our identity, not who we are. It's all part of the trance of unworthiness.

Our sorrow, guilt, and rage are trailheads, demarking where we can start. My own work around race and gender has been so healing because it's given my latent, unfelt emotions validity. This has opened up pathways for me to experience what was previously hidden in my body, heart, and mind.

The process has often been rocky, but that rockiness is a lot like the other tough stuff we encounter as we decide to prioritize Aliveness over the numb, default life. It's a hard, but it passes — and it's worth it. Slowly but surely, the Loop of Aliveness spins: we gain access to our curiosity, feel new frontiers of our body, access the powerful charge of our inner truths, and allow ourselves to live a more true life.

I've come to believe that, if we're interested in Aliveness, exploring the terrain of social identity is essential.

26

THE MAP IS NOT THE
TERRITORY

THE AUTUMN BREEZE blew through my hair from the open
window. It was late September 2008, but I didn't mind the
midnight San Jose chilliness as I drove home after an evening
with some dear friends. The night was a perfect mix of silly
jokes and deep conversation. I was feeling so at peace that I
was driving in silence, listening to the wind and feeling my
breath.

As I made my way east on Montague Expressway to my
parent's house, I stopped at a red light. Lazily, casually, with
complete nonchalance — I looked out my window.

What happened next defies description. Some inner metaphysical puzzle piece seemed to click into place, and I felt the
car, the pavement, and the building nearby *as me*. For a few
moments, if you had asked, the thing I would have identified
as "I" would have been all the stuff of the physical world
around me.

It was a first glimmer of truth, of touching the vision of reality
that Zen and so many other aptly-named "non-dual" spiritual
teachings try to articulate in countless ways. *Non-dual* is a

helpful pointer — deep down, there is no separation between self and other, between us and everything around us, between you and me.

Each of us, in our own way, has likely tasted some flavor of this oneness. It is the ground of our experience, in Zen called the *absolute* reality (as opposed to *relative* reality in which we experience ourselves as separate beings).

Having the Loop of Aliveness as a model has served me, and I continue to return to it and experiment with it in my life. When I'm stuck, it gives me a place to start, to enter the stuckness directly rather than trying to avoid it. It offers a way to shift my orientation, get back on track, or knock something loose as needed.

But a treasure map is only a piece of paper. We can never fully know our lives with words, ideas, and models. As such, I could not close this section without muddying the water in an attempt to make things more clear.

LOOPS IN A STRANGE LOOP

The Loop of Aliveness is actually a "strange loop" (from Douglas Hofstadter's classic book, *Gödel, Escher, Bach*). It's fundamentally paradoxical, non-linear, and interdependent. Just like the *yin* and *yang* symbol in which there is a small circle of black in the white half and vice versa, each of the four facets of the loop *contains* the others.

You could focus all your attention on any one of the four steps, and the other three would all come to life on their own. Keep getting curious in the present moment and you'll automatically end up in your body, feeling the charge of your life, and allowing it to unfold. You may have noticed this in the stories I shared — despite appearing in a chapter on one part of the Loop, included elements from each of them.

And when we travel the whole Loop and arrive back at inner curiosity, we find our experience and understanding of curiosity itself is transformed — it's larger than we could have ever imagined, yet it's still simply inner curiosity. We find ourselves back where we started, but we experience "where we started" in a new light.

There's an element of play and intuition that runs through the loop, a non-linearity and weirdness, a synchronicity and, dare I say, a divine whisper. Because change is the only constant in life, mystery is the essence of Aliveness. So, all the ways we foist linearity onto our experience are, in a subtle sense, *out of sync with reality itself* (including this Loop that I've been prattling on about). In the same way that a map is not real, even though the territory it describes is, the Loop is a helpful model but not, in the most profound sense, *true*.

From cutting-edge quantum physics to the depths of spiritual insight from mystics across traditions to anyone who has explored an altered mind state with deep presence, this much is clear: *Reality is fundamentally weird.*

The purpose of the Loop of Aliveness is not to put this weirdness in order but rather to keep us mentally safe as we travel more deeply into the mystery of our lives. Hopefully, when we encounter its inherent strangeness, we can freak out a little less and dance with it a little more.

Now that we've explored the Loop, I want to share the pillars of how I live it every day, how I keep myself "freaking out a little less and dancing a little more." They're the practical details of how I live my Vow: a seasonal prioritization ritual and daily check-in, various awareness and contemplative practices, and spending time in spaces and communities that encourage and reflect Aliveness.

PART IV

LIVING THE VOW

In the day-to-day trenches of adult life, there is no such thing as atheism, as not worshipping. Everybody worships. The only choice we get is what to worship.
David Foster Wallace

When you make the mind your friend,
you'll know what trust really means.
Listen. I have followed this path of friendship to its end.
And I can say with absolute certainty –
it will lead you home.
Mitta — *The Therigatha*, poems from the first Buddhist nuns

Today's enlightenment is tomorrow's delusion.
Hogen Sensei (my teacher)

THE EVERPRESENT VOW

"THESE SIXTEEN PRECEPTS have been handed down by the original Buddha, generation after generation through time, to me. Now, I give them to you. Will you maintain them well?"

My teacher's gaze pierced through me. No ounce of lie, falsehood, or inauthenticity was possible in this moment. Mustering every ounce of commitment in my heart, I responded, "I will."

Again, he asked: "Will you maintain them well?"

"I will.

"Will you maintain them well?"

I felt the gaze of the fifty or so people in the Temple bearing down on me.

"I will."

I had just completed a weeklong retreat in which I handsewn a *rakusu*, an intricate bib-like garment that represents an aspiring student's commitment to live by the Zen code of ethics and conduct. In the tight quarters of Fire Lotus Temple in Brooklyn with my teacher and two other students, I spent the week meditating, sewing, and diving deep into Zen teachings. At the end of the week, in this ceremony, we took *Jukai*, formally receiving and vowing to uphold the moral teachings of the Zen tradition, called the precepts.

The precepts represent a lifelong commitment to Zen and the path of spiritual training it lays out. They are not rules or commandments but rather a pledge to express the truth, compassion, and energy that comes from meditation and insight. By the time I received the precepts on that humid Brooklyn morning in early August 2023, I had no qualms in my heart. It was simply another aspect of my Vow of Aliveness.

The ceremony of *Jukai* has a second part: the receiving of one's *dharma* name. (*Dharma* is the Sanskrit word for Buddhist teaching.) Once a student receives a *dharma* name, the rest of the community calls the student by that name, and, more deeply, the name represents a lifelong teaching for the student.

My teacher turned to me, and I stepped forward and bowed. "I give you the name Baikei, which means "Cultivating Prajna" and comes from two Chinese characters. The second character, kei, is a Chinese character for the Sanskrit word *prajna* which describes the unification of the self with the absolute. Prajna is wisdom beyond wisdom, the direct experience of reality as it is. Bai, the first character, means cultivating, referring to cultivating the soil to give crops. Prajna is the ultimate aim of practice and, even when attained, is never completed. The best approach to fostering it is the most basic one: letting go, completely, in body and mind. Baikei, Cultivating Prajna."

Immediately, I understood both sides of this name — it was what I had already been doing and what I must do, an exhortation to continue, strengthen, and intensify my training, but to never forget to root myself in letting go.

Letting go is the essence. All of our ways of thinking and being — the habits accumulated over a lifetime in the default world — can be let go of. We can live our whole lives from the fresh source of Aliveness that flows within us, and the Vow of Aliveness is the container that allows for this.

VOW AS PROTECTION

Almost exactly 10 years ago, I stood in front of the Dalai Lama and took the Bodhisattva Vow for the first time while on my magical backpacking trip. In the decade that had passed, I had found a teacher and lineage to study with, moved to New York and then home to San Francisco, and made Zen the centerpoint of my life.

My Vow of Aliveness began to come into being in Dharamsala; it crystallized on that summer morning in Brooklyn. In the months that followed, I reflected on how I wanted to carry this Vow into the future. What did it mean to me? How was I going to live it? What role was it playing in my life?

In a talk my teacher gave shortly after *Jukai*, he referenced a quote by the Buddha: "Protect your mind like the bulwark protects a castle."

I had heard this teaching before, but I never liked it. Something about the word "protect" threw me off. The energy of "protection" felt tight and constrained, seemingly at odds with the openness of liberation.

But this time, when I heard my teacher's words, I understood. The default world always stands ready to devour us whole — my mind constantly needs protection. In fact, I already knew this. I had been filling my life with forms of protection: taking vows, meditating, returning to ZMM regularly, and so on. My new *dharma* name (which took me a while to embrace) has become part of this process, part of how I'm called back into my truth amidst the winds of the default world.

Each of these are, in essence, the Loop of Aliveness brought to life. Living my Vow means weaving this Loop into *everything* — from how I direct my attention in seemingly small, insignificant moments to how I make big, life-changing decisions. There are three core ways I do this that we'll explore over the final chapters of this book:

First are the seasonal prioritization ritual and daily check-in, which I created for myself with Emmye's support as I was building Awaken. They're essentially checkpoints in which I take a step back and consciously prioritize what's essential in my life, relying on presence and intuition more than left-brain logic. Each seasonal (or quarterly, i.e. changing of the seasons) prioritization ritual involves reflecting on how things have been going and naming what I want to do, how I want to live, and who I want to be. Then, for 15 minutes each morning (and a couple minutes longer on Mondays), I feed these priorities into my weekly goals and my daily schedule.

Second, I've assembled practices that help me grow my capacity for Aliveness. My goal with these is to find ways to turn everyday moments towards receiving the various flavors of Aliveness that they're offering me.

Third, I've prioritized specific spaces and communities that value Aliveness. First and foremost, obviously, is Zen Mountain Monastery and the month I spend there each year (including 2-3 week-long silent meditation retreats). I also go to Burning Man regularly, but the list doesn't stop here. Countercultural communities come in all shapes and sizes and provide an incredible antidote to the default world, whether we travel to them or cultivate them at home. They're places where we can explore the edges of our Aliveness and be inspired by those around us within a safe container — and, in the process, find and create deep relationships with fellow travelers on the path of Aliveness.

Ultimately, these are all just my ways of living and protecting my Vow, and I'm sharing them to inspire you to find rituals, practices, and spaces that support your own Aliveness.

28

PRIORITIZATION AS RITUAL

THE DOORBELL RANG, and I apprehensively answered it. It was one of my closest friends, Austin, and he walked in with a big smile on his face. "I've been looking forward to this." I nodded, returning his smile and feeling my nervousness thaw.

Over the next 15 minutes, four other friends arrived, and we sat down to begin. It was late December 2023. The year was drawing to a close, and we were gathered to reflect, embody, and dream into where we would point our energy in 2024. I had led these workshops in the past, but this was the first time I was doing them in-person.

Over the next 5 hours, we dove deep, sharing some of our highs and lows from the past year and allowing Aliveness to guide us toward what we wanted to prioritize going forward. Over the next few weeks, I would repeat this gathering with almost a hundred people (after fine-tuning the agenda so that it was shorter). I saw firsthand what a life-changing impact it had on nearly everyone who showed up.

In a sense, it's obvious and almost funny. Who knew that taking time to think about what's actually meaningful could have such a positive effect on how we live?

Yet, most of us live life on the fly, yolo-ing (in a default, non-alive way) each day, week, and month, moving from one thing to the next without giving much attention to how and where we're directing our energy. In moments of self-honesty, perhaps we get a glimpse into the vast chasm between how we've been living and our true life. Seeing this, we ping-pong between avoidance and shame. So often, it feels hard to reflect on how we've been living.

Practice is what solves this conundrum. Each quarter, in addition to seeing how I've fallen short, I also see how far I've come. As a meandering, iterative process, I move closer and closer to living in harmony and deep connection with my Inner World.

Do these rituals. As far as I can tell, there is no way to center Aliveness without something like them within default world life. Unless we're living in a monastery or some other place that systematically prioritizes *life*, we are going to get pulled off track by the forces around us. What makes these rituals so powerful is that they help us notice this is happening and bring us into alignment with what's truly meaningful for us.

KNOW WHERE YOU'RE GOING

Two rituals are at the center of my Vow of Aliveness: a quarterly deep dive and a daily standup. Both are inspired by the pillars of product management that served me so well at work: quarterly goal setting, sprint planning, daily standups, and retrospectives. Done together, these rituals give my life concrete roadmaps that are both spiritual and practical. They're regular checkpoints for reflection and integration.

The deep dive is focused on looking at the central questions of my life: Looking back, how have things actually been going? What did I want to emphasize last quarter, and how did that pan out?

Then, looking forward, what do I want to prioritize? What's going to be impactful at work? What am I hoping to cultivate in my meaningful relationships? What skills, hobbies, or projects do I want to spend time with? Where are my energy levels, and what does my body need? Most fundamentally, where in my life am I feeling most alive, and how can I nurture that Aliveness?

How we live into these questions basically determines our whole life. Taking time to sit with them has, for me and the folks I've done this with, been game-changing.

The daily standup is a fifteen-minute morning check-in where I take all of these big-picture answers and funnel them into an actionable plan for each week (on Mondays) and, on each weekday, a tangible schedule that'll help me *actually live* the priorities that are important to me. This process allows us to shrink the universe of things that are meaningful to us into something manageable, so we can quickly and easily set our priorities for each week and day.

Essentially, we're setting up quarters/seasons as bookends for our lives, creating containers where we can know which way we're going and commit to being present without reevaluation of our direction. This focuses our attention. As an example, if I'm not careful, I can spend months deliberating on whether to stay in a particular job. Instead of falling into this trap, the seasonal deep dive helps me figure out how I'm going to show up within the context of the job — how much of my energy I want it to take, how to make and hold boundaries, and what I actually want to get out of the job. Then, the daily standup helps me stick to these intentions.

After a defined period of time (usually a quarter, but you can always set it shorter or longer), I look back and evaluate. Was I able to find balance and enjoyment in my work, or did the environment overwhelm my intentions? Usually, the structure makes it easy to know I gave it an honest chance and therefore allows me to stay or leave with clarity. The structure gives me the confidence to put my energy towards what I'm going to do differently instead of second-guessing my choices.

I want to offer three other invitations as part of the rituals. First, everything here is just an idea — use it as a starting point to create the rituals that you're excited to do within *your* life. Second, experiment with doing the rituals with the people in your life. This lays the groundwork for richer connection as we share our reflections and aspirations with each other. It's also a great way to overcome the inertia that sometimes causes us to avoid doing the work of getting honest with ourselves. Third, bring the seasons into this ritual: host a comfy, cozy deep dive gathering with hot cocoa in the winter, do it over a picnic in the summer sun.

The rituals are rooted in the Loop of Aliveness: we start with reflection questions and inner curiosity. From there, our core action is to *embody*, to come into presence physically, and then to feel what flavors of truth or charge arise. Finally, we *allow* our Inner World to speak to us, to take us where it will and guide our path with its wisdom. In short, we're uncovering aspects of our Inner World and using our intuition to understand how we might let these aspects flow into how we live our lives.

THE PRIORITIES: VIBES, GOALS, IDENTITIES

The inner exploration we do during the deep dive ritual focuses on distilling what's alive for us into three core categories: Vibes, Goals, and Identities. These are labels that give shape to what we encounter in our Inner World, pointers that we carry with us into the daily standup and throughout our life.

VIBES

Vibes represent what we want to feel — how we want to experience life. They name the feeling state that we're looking to invoke and cultivate. Some examples are spaciousness, harmony, excitement, or love. Usually, they respond to our circumstances — if we've been feeling rushed, perhaps the vibe we're yearning for is spaciousness or rest.

Life obviously won't always feel like our desired vibe, but it gives us a feeling-tone that we can cultivate. We notice when our vibes are present and, in doing so, learn about the conditions that allow them to arise. A life rooted in the right vibes keeps us open and curious, helping us choose and stay within the Loop of Aliveness instead of getting caught in distraction and dissociation.

The reason vibes come first in the deep dive is that they have the power to guide the rest of the process. We spend lots of time worrying about the practical details of our lives — our schedule, the types of things we buy or eat, or anything else. But when we're in contact with our vibe, we don't need to worry about those things as much.

A great example of this happened on a random Sunday this past spring. My vibe for the season was creativity, and I had two invitations for the day: one to a dear friend's birthday and second for a creative workshop that another good friend was leading at her brand new art studio.

A younger me might have worried about what to do. It was clear which option would nourish my creativity, but what about the social dynamics of it all? I wanted to attend the workshop, but guilt probably would have coerced me into going to the birthday.

But that's not what happened. I called up my birthday friend — with whom I'm very close — and told him about the workshop and that I couldn't come. I made sure he knew how much he meant to me as a friend and set a date to take him out to lunch the next week. Perhaps due to my candor, he didn't feel neglected by me not coming — he totally understood and was inspired by it.

I felt this decision as a low-key magical process. My clarity on vibe made it obvious what I wanted to prioritize. My friend even mentioned an arts space nearby that he wanted to visit and asked if I wanted to go with him some time. When we live authentically and directly like this, it's contagious.

GOALS

Goals are the most straightforward of the three priorities. A goal is anything we want to accomplish. It's a vision of a world that does not yet exist — and when we see this not-yet-existing world, it gives us inspiration and energy to create it. The right goals help us stay embodied and channel charge into action.

A well-articulated goal generally answers some key questions: What are you going to do? When will it get done? How will you know when it's done? Who else will be involved?

There are countless goal-setting frameworks out there, such as SMART goals (Specific, Measurable, Achievable, Realistic, and Time-bound) goals, OKRs (Objectives and Key Results), HARD goals (Heartfelt, Animated, Required, and Difficult), and more. Maybe you want to get specific by listing dates, milestones, etc. using SMART goals, or perhaps it helps to group your goals in a logical fashion like the OKR framework does. It's just about doing what enables you to feel organized and inspired.

There's plenty of info about these various frameworks online, so go deeper if you're curious. These days, I like HARD the best (mainly because of the "H"), so if it helps, you're welcome to try it on:

•Heartfelt — the goal matters to you; you can feel its meaning in your life, its resonance within your Inner World.

•Animated — like being heartfelt, when you bring the goal to mind, it gives you energy.

•Required — you have to do it. Not as some sort of obligation, but as an inner knowing of requirement. There was no logical reason nor outer pressure for me to write this book. Yet, in an inner sense, it was required.

•Difficult — the goal has the right level of challenge, bringing you to your edge (in a helpful, *alive* way).

Experiment with these various methods of goal setting as you do the rituals, but be sure to check in with what feels good. Honestly, I've felt mixed about goals my whole life. In large part, this is because I'm more of a means-over-ends person — I find that if I'm overly focused on the ends, I get disconnected from the present and start to rush, doing things with a frantic edge to my energy.

Beyond that, goals can have a propensity to backslide into unhelpful self-critique. If I'm overly identified with achieving goals, I'm going to feel deflated and even ashamed when I inevitably don't reach some of them. Don't set goals that are rooted in pressure and shame, but if this happens, know that it's just part of the learning process.

The best goals promote presence and clarity across our lives. Remember, goals serve Aliveness — not the other way around.

IDENTITIES

When I got back from that walk where I realized I wanted to write this book, I tried saying to myself, "I am a writer," and I had a mini internal explosion. My insides screamed — I was excited, scared, nervous, all at the same time. I could feel a powerful charge flowing through my body — alive, juicy, and edgy.

When people asked about my job over the next quarter, I answered, "I'm a writer." Just saying these words filled me with a sense of empowerment, making the project even more real for me.

I was living into a vision of who I was, and doing this was giving me tangible energy. In other seasons, we might not have this sort of vision, but when we look at our goals or our vibes, something emerges. In either case, identity can be one of our life's most profound north stars, pointing us to who we're becoming in this chapter of our life and unlocking our Aliveness in the process.

In trying on an identity for a season, we're feeling what's alive, noticing where our blocks are, and just experimenting with curiosity and openness. Within the Loop of Aliveness, we're *allowing* an inner truth to start to become an outer identity and seeing how it feels.

There's power in this. Had I not permitted myself to identify as a writer, this book would be very different or, more likely, not have been written at all. It felt incredibly empowering to identify as "a writer," and now there's a book that you're reading. That's all I need to know to trust this sort of intuition and the magic of consciously choosing identities.

PUTTING IT TOGETHER

Taken together, vibes, goals, and identities have an orienting power that cuts through the distractions, habits, and pressures we come across in the default world.

The rituals give us space to set our priorities consciously. The full specifics of both rituals are in the appendix, the basics are quite simple: During the quarterly deep dive, we brainstorm and select 3 of each of the priorities (vibes, goals, and identities). These serve as a guide for the season, and we return to them regularly. Then, in the daily standup, we narrow these down into three weekly goals and one vibe that we use to help schedule each day.

One of my friends who attended the most recent deep dive mentioned she wrote her priorities out and pasted them on her bathroom mirror as a way of keeping them in mind. Then, she read them over each morning as she prepared for her day.

Personally, I use a Google doc template for these rituals, making a copy for each season and keeping it open in a browser tab for frequent revisiting. I also host open, free, online gatherings to do the deep dives together quarterly, and I'd love for you to join! For an invite when these happen and a link to the templates, simply sign up for my newsletter or visit my website:

29

TRAINING IN ALIVENESS

WHILE BACKPACKING IN 2013, I was absorbed in spiritual or mindfulness practice almost all day. From wandering to riding trains and buses to sitting and having a coffee and talking to strangers, I was experiencing each thing I did as an opportunity to just be present.

Coming back from the trip, I found myself enmeshed in the default world before I even knew what hit me. My mind was constantly trying to plan or mentally manage every remote situation and possibility in my free moments. I noticed how frequently I was choosing to bury my attention in my phone or some other form of stimulation and consumption. The openness and delightful aimlessness were almost completely gone.

Seeing this was a turning point. I understood why *training* was the word used to describe embarking on the Buddhist path — and why I *needed* training if I was going to keep the fire of Aliveness lit.

That meant I needed to answer practical, fundamental questions. How was I going to wait for and ride the subway? How did I want to navigate my relationship to substances? Who did I want to hang out with? How was I going to lay out my living space?

In essence, what was I going to do and how was I going to live to make it easier to choose Aliveness rather than living on autopilot?

The following practices are my favorite ways of trying to do this. I came up with some of them, but all draw inspiration from teachers and teachings that I've been fortunate enough to encounter.

Most of them have three basic steps: First, each practice has an anchor of some sort, and we place our attention on this anchor (like the breath in meditation). Second, when our attention slips away and we find ourselves wondering what we're going to cook tonight or mentally sorting through our todo list, *all we need to do is notice*. Third and most importantly, after noticing we've gotten distracted, we simply come back to the anchor of our practice.

The second and third steps represent a potential pitfall and a vital opportunity. It can be so easy to get lost in the infinite versions of the "I can't do this" thought. We can instinctively think this thought is true because it describes what we just experienced. The idea here is to recognize this sort of thinking as *just another thought* — just mind-noise that we can let go of and come back to the attention anchor.

Furthermore, many of the practices bring us to an inner edge, a place in which we're a bit uncomfortable. Play with your sense of edge as you go through them, making sure to take care of yourself by not going out *past* your edge.

For example, we see this dynamic in the practice of working out. Some people loathe the discomfort of working out and never do it. Others blow past their limits and work out too much, making it an obsession and causing themselves injuries or health problems. Practice is rooted in finding a balance between these two extremes.

Finally, the practices I'm sharing are less traditional, ones I've evolved or borrowed for navigating my own life. My primary practice is *zazen* (zen meditation), but for that and many others (yoga, stretching, etc.), there are plenty of resources out there that offer far more depth than I could. Instead, I'm focusing on how I take Aliveness off the meditation cushion and the yoga mat. I highly recommend having a traditional core practice — something you commit to daily and train in more formally. But aside from that, I hope you enjoy these practices and what they bring to your life.

EMBODIED AWARENESS

Embodying is the second/"action" part of the Loop of Aliveness — placing the attention on and in the body. As such, it's a potent skill. With training, all of us have the ability — in any moment — to move from circular, distracted, or anxious thinking into body awareness.

When we embody, we encounter the physical sensations of our emotional states, and the practices below are containers for feeling and staying with these sensations. Over time, meeting our energy at the physical, embodied level (rather than in thinking) becomes much an easier and more healing way of navigating tough moments (and a more ecstatic way of experiencing joyful ones).

Rest practice

Ironically, I learned how to rest from *sesshin*. The weeklong retreats are intense and grueling, but each afternoon, around

45 minutes are set aside for rest. This rest is necessary — I usually sleep only 4-5 hours per night while doing intensive practice. This dynamic sets up an interesting conundrum: I need to get into a rested, nourishing state as quickly as I can.

It's been a fantastic skill to hone over the years. I practice rest every day. It's the most fundamental form of self-care that I can imagine. I set a timer, lie down, and feel the earth underneath me. To facilitate this, sometimes I do a body scan or rest my attention on my breath, but the core of the practice is letting my body feel heavy and supported by the ground. Sometimes I sleep, sometimes I don't — I don't give it much thought one way or another.

We have so much conditioning that can make deep rest hard — trying to maximize our experience, a check-the-box productivity mindset, an unworthiness of doing absolutely nothing, and more. In the modern world, rest is one of those practices that seems simple but is actually one of the most profound things we can do.

Working out

I want to frame working out both as a practice of embodiment *and* charge. The embodiment part is straightforward — in physical exercise, we bring our attention to the feeling of the body and the muscles as we move. But beyond that, it's actually one of my favorite practices for feeling my emotional charge in the body.

One example of this is almost a cliche: anger or even rage. Working out in this way is one of the few socially acceptable expressions of these emotions. This can get unhealthy when taken to an extreme, but as a technique for letting off some steam, it's actually quite helpful. My sister took up boxing a few years ago, and I've seen how it's a fantastic outlet for her, a workout within which she can safely feel and express anger. She's palpably more relaxed after her training sessions.

But working out as a practice of feeling our bodies and emotions doesn't stop at anger — there are infinite flavors of emotion that can be experienced and expressed in working out.

Here's how it functions: the act of working out takes us to an edge within our physical capacity. At this edge, our body is straining to do an activity, and our habitual holding and tightness start to loosen, simply because that holding is restricting our ability to give our full energy to the workout. To make that more tangible, if I'm straining to do a few more pushups, I'm just not going to have the energy to clench my neck and shoulder muscles in the way I usually do. This loosening opens up a pathway to feel what is underneath some of the habitual tension I'm often carrying around.

I feel this so clearly when I run up the hill in nearby Buena Vista Park. It's strenuous, requiring me to be single-minded in effort as I get close to the top. In these moments, as I feel myself giving my whole being to the act of running, I notice a huge range of emotions and energies spilling out and coming to the surface.

One of the most common of these is body anxiety — a jittery feeling that is usually locked away within habitual tension (and experienced as mental anxiety). As I'm going all-in trying to run up the hill, this energy spills out into my being.

And within this, magic happens. It's like the anxiety *becomes* the running. The jitteriness gets channeled into keeping me running, a primal scream that powers my vigorous effort. When I get to the top, I feel a calm and presence, having embodied and processed some of this habitual anxiety.

Working out offers a particularly useful container for this to happen. As we're pushed to our physical edge, we have a unique window to feel the emotion and charge present there.

Listening to music

When was the last time you just listened to music? Not while doing dishes or running or commuting or anything else — *just listened*?

That's the core of this practice — giving ourselves the time and space to do so. We direct our attention to the sensation of sound and allow it to be a meditative anchor, listening with our whole body.

For me, this is a lifeline to embodiment, relaxation, and pleasure. I put on an album that I love and lie down, sit quietly, or sing along, allowing myself to become the joy of music and relaxation.

Embodied Eating

For so many of us, eating is a multi-tasked activity — rarely do we sit down and just eat a meal. The practice here is to do just that, and ideally to do it in silence, so you can tune into your body, tasting the food and feeling the nourishment it offers.

This can be practiced at any time, and can even be done with people. At Zen Mountain Monastery, many meals are eaten in silence for this reason.

But if it feels too weird to do for a full meal, try doing it for just the first five minutes of a meal. When I'm with friends who want to try it, we set a timer for five minutes and eat in silence, tasting the food with full attention. Then, once the timer goes off, we return to regular conversation and eating — and usually, people are so intrigued by their experience of eating in silence that it becomes the topic of conversation. There is so much *taste* we typically miss.

Chris's menu salivating

Over dinner a few months ago, I told my friend Chris Palmer about my story of picking where to go to lunch. Instantly, he lit up and said he does something similar when he's choosing what to eat at a restaurant.

He looks at the menu and reads it slowly. As he's reading, he notices which items cause him to salivate. When he feels himself salivating, he orders that item.

He proceeded to do it live (as we were about to order), and it was awesome to see him use such a simple and embodied technique to navigate such a regular life situation, one that we can sometimes overthink. This simple practice *is* inner curiosity, embodied in a straightforward way.

Embodying difficult emotions

My friend, Stix, shared this practice with me, and I fell in love with it right away. The background is that, in early March 2020, Stix's partner broke up with him, and because they shared a living space, Stix had to move out. That same week, he was fired from his job.

Obviously, this double whammy would have been disorienting and heartbreaking by itself. He was able to crash at a friend's place, sleeping on a couch in the backyard (with a covering over it, fortunately). But the next week, the pandemic shut everything down, and his options for housing and jobs almost all vanished.

It was, to say the least, an anxiety-inducing situation. So every morning, when he felt the anxiety creeping in, he set a 15 minute timer and, for that time, allowed himself to *feel it all* — to think whatever thoughts, make whatever sounds, move his body (and punch his pillow) however he wanted.

Things ended up working out. Eventually, Stix found a long-term place to stay, and he's now in a wonderful relationship. He attributes the grace with which he navigated his situation to his morning anxiety practice.

This makes total sense to me, and when I heard it, I instantly asked him if I could include it in this book. It's a perfect example of the whole Loop of Aliveness:

First, the trigger of anxiety didn't distract him — instead, it pulled him into getting curious about what was going on inside rather than instinctively avoiding it. Second, he decided to *embody* the anxiety (embodying being the core of the practice). In doing so, he was choosing to *feel* the charge of anxiety rather than subtly avoiding it. This allowed the energy to be expressed and therefore move through his system.

When you notice there is a significant emotion or energy within your experience, see if it helps to give yourself time each day to simply *feel, embody, and express* that emotion. Set a timer and invite it to come out however it wants. When I know I'm dealing with a dominant emotion that seems to be sticking around, I do this practice every day for a few weeks, giving myself a chance to regularly connect with and feel the emotion.

In a slow and steady way, this practice can be life-changing.

LIFESTYLE

These practices include embodiment, but I call them "life-style" practices because they involve setting up our lives so that we more often choose the Loop of Aliveness and less frequently slip into habits of distraction and numbness. Individually, they're just small, everyday ways that empower us to be more alive, but collectively they (and countless other practices like it that we can create for ourselves) help us center Aliveness in *how we live*.

Watching TV and breathing

I don't watch a ton of TV, but when I do, I usually start by setting an intention that I want to pay attention to my body while watching. I practice giving roughly 10% of my attention to the breath. That is, I'll watch TV as normal, but I'll keep coming back to the sensation of breathing in a background sort of way.

What's so interesting about this is that I get to more intimately feel how my body reacts to what's on the television. If I'm excited or sad, I get to feel those emotions as body sensations with a little more clarity than I otherwise would.

It also gives me a better sense of what I actually like. I may think I like a particular show for, say, the action scenes. When I'm doing this practice, though, I notice that those action scenes make my body feel exhilarated. It's the feeling of exhilaration that I really like, and the action scenes are a means to stimulate this feeling.

This practice makes watching TV more *satisfying*. Just like knowing when I'm full after eating, I tend to have a clearer sense of when the activity is finished and make a healthier decision about when to get up.

. . .

Making distractions less accessible

I stumbled upon this practice more than a decade ago, as I found my relationship to alcohol changing. I used to drink quite a bit when I was in college. As I got older and started practicing meditation, my desire to drink went down dramatically. But sometimes, an old habit energy would get stirred up, and I'd find myself reaching for a drink when I didn't really want one. Almost before I knew it, I'd be having a beer.

In my late 20s, I found a novel solution to dealing with this: putting the alcohol out of reach. I put beer in the back of the fridge, so I'd have to take everything out to access it. I put whiskey above the cabinets, so I'd need to climb onto a chair and move other items I had in storage there just to reach it.

It was, in essence, using the power of friction to guide behavior. Pouring a thimble of whiskey was no longer a simple activity, but one that I needed to do a little work for. If I was willing to do this 30-second task to have a drink, I would just let myself drink. It removed the impulsivity of the act and forced me to do something embodied, a process that naturally stirs reflection.

This behavior hack worked, and I found myself drinking even less frequently — and, more importantly, drinking when I genuinely wanted to rather than mindlessly following an impulse.

I rarely drink these days, so this practice has faded away, but I continue to use the tactic of adding friction when it makes sense. For example, I've blocked Reddit on my regular web browser, so I'm forced to open a different browser when I want to access the website.

Try this out in the context of your own life. For example, leave your phone in one place instead of carrying it around your living space, and get an alarm clock (or use an old phone) so you don't need to keep it by your bed at night. Simply by making our distractions harder to access, we open up space for us to dwell in Aliveness much more often.

Artist dates

Artist Dates are originally from the popular book, *The Artist's Way* by Julia Cameron. I'll let her share the method:

"An artist date is a block of time, perhaps two hours weekly, especially set aside and committed to nurturing your creative consciousness, your inner artist. In its primary form, the artist date is an excursion, a play date that you pre-plan and defend against all interlopers. You do not take anyone on this artist date but you and your inner artist, a.k.a. your creative child. That means no lovers, friends, spouses, children — no taggers-on of any stripe. Doing your artist date, you are receiving — opening yourself to insight, inspiration, and guidance."

Here are a few of my regular Artist Dates:

- Rollerblading through Golden Gate Park down to Ocean Beach
- Going to a play, movie, or concert
- Having dinner and taking a stroll through a different neighborhood
- Heading down to Fisherman's Wharf and reliving childhood memories of visiting the city with my family
- Reading a book or writing at a bar or coffee shop

- Going on a hike in the redwoods or down by the ocean

You get the point. Artist dates are something that I love doing, where I can immerse myself in the experience and notice what makes me feel alive. They're a goldmine for cultivating inner curiosity and seeing what's alive in the Inner World.

Waiting

Waiting is truly one of the most radical and accessible practices in these times. We are *constantly* avoiding waiting. For or on the bus or train, in traffic, at the doctor's office or restaurant — the opportunities to *just wait* are countless.

But mostly, we don't take them as opportunities to wait — we distract ourselves. So, the practice of waiting is to identify these moments as they arrive in your life and simply wait.

This is still a challenging practice for me. I want to be productive and don't want to just "waste" the time. Taking 5 minutes to respond to days-old texts seems like a good use of the downtime that pops up.

This discomfort and impulse towards productivity (or away from boredom, another common reaction that comes up in these situations) is a fantastic ground to *just feel* what's going on inside.

So next time you have to wait for something, put away the phone and the music or podcast and *just wait*. Each time you notice yourself wanting to turn that waiting time *into* something, let that go, and just come back to waiting, using waiting as a means to get curious about what's going on inside.

. . .

Random walks

Random walks are a bit like Artist Dates, but they're shorter and, for me, a staple practice for unplugging from the day-to-day grind and connecting with myself. I leave my apartment and just wander. Each time I come to an intersection or need to choose which way to go, I survey the surroundings and listen inside to see what answer arises, which direction is calling me. During my backpacking trip, I did this all day, walking 15 or 20 miles and seeing parts of places like Istanbul or Cairo that I would have never been to otherwise.

My short, everyday random walks are 10-15 minute jaunts around my neighborhood. When I have more time, I'll go to a different part of town and just take in the streets, landscapes, parks, etc.

Leaning on your favorite things

I read *The Alchemist* each year and keep *The War of Art* next to my desk or on my bed stand. I Youtube the occasional Lord of the Rings clip before I start writing and, yes, I have listened to *Hamilton* on runs throughout the past year. There's much more on this list of things that inspire me: specific episodes of *Avatar: The Last Airbender*, *Sister Outside* by Audre Lorde, *Changes* or *Keep Ya Head Up* by Tupac, Sufjan Stevens' album *Illinois*, the last scene of *Apollo 13*, and many others.

I keep these magic potions close. All of us, I hope, have certain stories or music that move us. These are gold; they connect us with the charge and Aliveness that lives within us.

Overly revisited, they can lose their potency. But used at appropriate moments, spending time with our favorite stuff can be the little nudge that connects us to emotional energies that are ripe for flowing.

We know how to do this. Breakup songs that let the tears flow are *profoundly* healing as we process the end of a relationship.

The same can hold true with location. While growing up, our family would take regular trips to Pier 39 in San Francisco. I fell in love with the magic and mystery of being by the water with the fog rolling in or the vast Pacific Ocean floating behind the majestic Golden Gate Bridge. A few times a year, when I'm looking for inspiration, I take myself on an artist date there and get in touch with my inner child.

Revisiting our favorite things as a practice involves *knowing when we want to explore an emotional energy* and then giving ourselves time and space to do so. Let yourself be immersed in the world of whatever you're taking in, and keep ~10% of your attention on your breath and body to stay connected to the physical sensations you're experiencing.

For me, this is a sacred practice. When the night is still and I put on Seal's *Kiss from a Rose*, I can feel the music touch the depths of my soul. What a wild, profound, and beautiful thing it is that this random song evokes such a deep reaction.

I don't listen to *Kiss from a Rose* casually. I don't put it on while I'm cleaning my apartment or going for a run (I mean, that would just be weird). I give it my full attention, allow it to penetrate my skin and bones, let it reverberate in my Inner World.

RELATIONAL

These practices either directly involve someone else or are rooted in the relational parts of our lives. Ultimately, we need the people around us to reflect and support our Aliveness, these practices are how I've helped cultivate Aliveness within my relationships. The doing part of these tends to focus on inner curiosity and embodiment, but given their complexity, the practices touch the entire of the Loop of Aliveness.

Cuddling

Cuddling is, without a doubt, my favorite embodiment practice. Obviously, this needs a partner (or multiple partners), and for many of us, that's someone we're romantically involved with. But that's not the only way to cuddle! Friends can be great cuddle partners! In many cities, there are even groups of people who meet up for non-romantic cuddling. I once dated someone who had several cuddle partners, and it was fascinating to hear about her experiences in New York's cuddling community.

The way I like to anchor in the practice of cuddling is by bringing my attention to the points of contact with the person I'm cuddling with — the places we're touching each other. Resting my attention in these points of contact, I then breathe and allow my body to relax, connecting with the feeling of support coming from the ground (the bed, sofa, or whatever is supporting me) and connection with the person next to me. A timer can help demarcate a start and end to the practice, but, of course, it's not necessary.

Consciously making time for this practice (and finding the right person or people to do it with) can be a wonderful way to embody and connect with others.

Eye gazing

With people we know and love, eye-gazing can be an incredibly connective and presencing practice. (I've also done it with strangers in various workshops, which is super interesting as well.)

Eye gazing is quite simple. Set your timer to a desired length of time, usually 2-5 minutes, and simply sit in silence and look into each other's eyes. Allow the body to rest, the eyes to relax, and self-consciousness to flow out.

From here, just notice what comes up. How does the body feel? The heart? What charge might be present?

Don't project too much into what you think you *should* feel. Just let it be a practice, and thank your partner when you're done.

Dyad practices

During the Undoing Patriarchy retreat (and in many other retreats and the rituals outlined earlier), we frequently did dyad practices, where we work with a prompt. For instance, one question was, "What messages of masculinity did you receive while growing up?"

In taking this up, one person speaks, and the other person simply listens. Sometimes, the speaker is allowed time to simply keep talking and see what comes out. Alternatively, you can give the listener a prescribed response — for example, each time the speaker completes an answer, the listener can say "thank you" and repeat the prompt, letting the speaker answer it multiple times as a way of seeing what comes out.

The idea is that, over time, your conscious, directing part of speaking turns off — you stop filtering your words and just speak, giving voice to your Inner World in an uninhibited way. So often, this practice can catalyze amazing personal insights.

Dyads can be used in many situations — I use them with friends and romantic partners when there's something we want to explore, either about our interpersonal dynamic or some part of our lives.

Pausing in conversation

Last year, I led a daylong product strategy offsite for the executive team of a startup that I was consulting for. This team has had a number of deep-rooted disagreements and communication difficulties, but they all truly want what's best for the company.

During the day, things would inevitably get heated. When this happened, I asked everyone to simply take a few moments to breathe, be silent, and feel whatever was coming up.

Each time we restarted the conversation, things would improve. The pause shifted the way people would communicate. Without my prompting, team members would automatically start by labeling their feelings: "I felt some fear when you talked about deadlines for next quarter." This is an inarguable statement that invites empathy, and sharing like this helped us get back on track throughout the offsite.

By the end of the day, members of their team were not only talking about how much they liked pausing, but proactively asking for pauses as needed!

Pausing is truly game-changing in relationships. So often, when things get difficult, we accelerate our activity and conversation. We talk faster, interrupt, and generally exert ourselves, whether it's to move things forward, express our emotions, or anything else. Rarely does this respond to the underlying emotional energy of the conflict at hand.

Instead, when we notice an interaction getting speedy or confrontational, we can ask whoever we're with to pause, to simply sit and be in silence and feel our bodies. This can feel daunting the first time, but as you practice it, it can become second nature, both in the context of a particular relationship and in all sorts of social situations. The concept of pausing was totally foreign to the startup that I was working with, and yet they quickly picked it up and ran with it.

One way to relieve some of the social pressure around pausing is to talk about it before a tricky conversation. With the heads-up already in place, it's usually easier to ask for a pause when you want one.

Pausing can also be used as a form of embodying enjoyment. Sometimes, a moment — in conversation or otherwise — can feel really good, and we can ask for a pause to simply be in that goodness with more presence and less worry about what to say or do next.

Perceiving and receiving love instead of getting triggered

I have a fantastic relationship with my parents. I love them dearly, and when we hang out, we genuinely enjoy each other's company.

But it wasn't always like this. We've had our fair share of fights, blow-ups, and storm-outs. I was definitely not the easiest kid and teenager, and some of my angstiness persisted through my 20s.

One of the main things that's shifted for me over the years is learning how to receive love from them — attuning myself to the ways they express love so I can recognize them in real time.

Here's a common example of a situation that's never easy: As of now, though I'm completely open to it, I'm not actively chasing the marriage-and-kids path. This is difficult for my parents to accept, especially as immigrants raised within Indian culture, in which having kids is the norm.

For many years, this had been an escalating push from them. Each time the topic came up, we'd get into an argument. We were caught between a rock and a hard place: I wanted one thing for my life, they wanted another, and the two were mutually incompatible.

Or so I thought. As my practice brought me deeper into my body and mind, I started to bring more awareness to these situations. I realized there were two key elements of what was going on: love and conditioning.

First and foremost, my parents were expressing love in their advice and desires. They wanted me to experience the joy of children and felt I might regret my decision if I didn't.

Second, there was conditioning. They were operating out of scripts of what life is supposed to include. I was responding to this energy with my own conditioning — teenage years of trying to assert my independence while also wanting my parents to love me and support my path. Like many parent-child relationships, there was a way in which our habit patterns ping-ponged off each other and led to friction and disconnection.

And I saw that, with practice, I could interrupt the ping-ponging of our conditioning, simply by focusing on the love. Each time the topic of kids came up, I would say to myself internally, "This is my parents expressing care and love." I'd try to *feel* this care as fully as I could in the moment with my whole body.

Turning outward, I'd respond by telling them that I hear them and understand their perspective. Then, I turned the conversation towards how much I love them, how grateful I am for them, and how meaningful our relationship is to me.

Only after this would I reiterate that I'm open to having kids, but not actively focused on it like many of my friends. Their response was much softer, and our conversations went much more smoothly.

Taking a moment to feel the love within their message of concern changed everything about both what I said and *how* I responded energetically. The love and care were magnified, and their concern became secondary. It helped them recenter in the reality that, whether I have kids or not, our relationship being loving and open is the most important thing.

It happened over a decade with persistent effort, but doing this practice resulted in a monumental breakthrough. The things that used to be annoying have been rewired inside me. Over the years, they've come to inquire about kids less, trusting that I'm living an intentional life. This is a challenging practice, to be sure, but it's real, and it's possible to do.

30

SPACES AND COMMUNITIES OF
ALIVENESS

YOU DON'T WALK by the giant prayer wheel without spinning it three times. This is one of the many unwritten rules I learned as I stayed in the remote mountain village of Lamayuru while attending a weeklong teaching on death and the *bardos*, the stages between this life and the next.

It was 2013, and I was on my backpacking trip, just a week away from starting my first solo retreat. Lamayuru is a small village with a population of a couple hundred people and is thoroughly Tibetan Buddhist in culture and customs. Prayer flags fluttered in the breeze everywhere I turned. On the main roads, there were small, backpack-sized cylindrical prayer wheels built into the mud-brick walls. At major intersections, of which there were just a few, the wheels were taller than me, with handles to help turn them.

Walking down the street, villagers would casually turn the small prayer wheels, like feeling a bush or tree as it moved past them. At corners, they'd stop and, as I mentioned, do three full turns, walking around the wheel while holding one of the handles. In their left hand, they generally had a *mala* (prayer beads), which they would finger through as they softly chanted *Om Mani Padme Hum*, the Lotus Jewel Mantra. When villagers encountered one another, there was always a "Juleh!" exchanged, a greeting of warmth and hello.

Can you imagine this scene in our Western world? Spinning toys everywhere and a fun-sounding chant you can repeat to get you out of your head? Warm greetings as you walked down the street. Anxiety would be hard to maintain in such a setting.

The smiles and eyes and relaxed gaits of the people in Lamayuru were some of the happiest of any place I had been. It was yet another moment of *wow, this stuff works*. Their culture might seem silly and quant to us *serious* Westerners, but they had clearly figured something out that was advanced beyond anything I had encountered.

EMBRACING THE COLLECTIVE

Environment matters. The experience of living the Ladakhi village life that week was the spark that lit the fuse of my desire to prioritize people and places that encouraged my Aliveness.

As a society, the West is dedicated to and rooted in the perspective of the individual, prioritizing it over the collective in countless ways. It's baked into the American Dream of owning a house with a white picket fence, metaphorically and literally cordoned off from the rest of the neighborhood and world.

Growing up, I saw firsthand how different this dynamic was in Indian communities. Generally speaking, in Indian households and culture, Western ideas like boundaries and personal space are deprioritized. Everyone is up in everyone else's business. It was frustrating, at times, growing up feeling like I didn't always have a lot of space from parents and relatives, and that all activities were defaulted to being done together.

But even back then, I could feel the upside of this way of being, the no-questions-asked generosity and reliability of family and friends. I saw how clearly the values emphasized by my parents were echoed and magnified within their group of friends (almost all Indian immigrants), forming a protective cocoon that seemed to surround me (and the other parents' children in the community).

Unbeknownst to my conscious mind, this aspect of my upbringing oriented me to community in a profound way. At no point did I consider my journey of Aliveness to be a solo endeavor. I purposefully sought out the people and communities from which I intuitively felt Aliveness resonate. From monasteries to social movements to the friends I chose, I allowed myself to be enveloped and taught by these spaces and the folks within them.

The energy of this enveloping is infectious and transformative. During the time I spend at the monastery, I feel the force field of the teachings, people, and our collective practice as a bulwark against distraction, anxiety, and numbness. Without cell phone service most of the time and surrounded by nature and practice, the days feel peaceful and still. Each time I return to San Francisco, I can feel myself bringing this tranquility back with me in a way that helps illuminate how I want to live and use my energy within my usual life.

STAYING ALIVE

Community is an essential part of living my Vow of Aliveness. I have found it impossible to hold the energy of Aliveness by myself. Without like-minded community, I inevitably slide into the perspectives and behaviors of the default world. If living the Vow involves protecting and guarding our minds (and hearts), there is strength in numbers.

Aside from the monastery, I also go to Burning Man most years. It's become an artistic pulse check on my life. The festival is clearly one of the most extraordinary and wild things I've ever experienced, and yet, having been so many times, it sometimes feels worn and familiar. A core Zen teaching involves cultivating "beginner's mind" (the title of Zen Master Shenryu Suzuki's famous book) — dropping our ideas and experiencing life with fresh eyes. The familiar-yet-out-there-ness of Burning Man is the perfect place to practice this. Inevitably, the creative spark I feel there so palpably in the art and humans nourishes my own.

Travel is another tool in my tool belt, whether it's going to India or a weekend camping trip in Northern California. Regardless of where we are, whatever ways we can get outside of our usual context can be helpful in connecting us with our true life.

And perhaps most importantly, we can find and create communities and spaces of Aliveness right where we live. When I moved home to San Francisco, I was fortunate to have a deep community already in place from high school and growing up. But as I reconnected with old friends, I found myself falling into default social patterns that I wanted to shift.

So, I began hosting quarterly deep dives and meditation gatherings and generally proactively created spaces that I felt encouraged Aliveness. In taking a more active role in shaping my social life, I've been able to reconnect with old friends in new ways and make new friends in the process. People whom I had no idea were meditators now text me to see if I want to join them at evening meditation practice at the nearby Zen center.

It's been a profoundly enlivening process. My relationships are even deeper and more intimate than I could have imagined when I returned home. These days, between deeply loving the Bay Area and climate considerations, joining and building community right where I am — rather than seeking it elsewhere — is one of my primary aims.

COMMITTING TO COMMUNITY

Try taking a look around at the people in your life — are they more often choosing curiosity or distraction? Embodiment or numbness? Truth or avoidance? Allowing or controlling? When I look around and am honest with myself, it's pretty easy to see where Aliveness is being cultivated and where it's being turned away from. The loop and its parts are a fantastic lens for understanding a space or new group of people when I encounter them.

When I find a community that nourishes my Aliveness, I commit to them in a non-evaluating way. I no longer question whether I should go to the monastery, even if a particular visit feels uninspiring or even difficult. I choose to stay, interpreting challenges as something to be worked with rather than turned away from.

This is hard, especially for most folks in the West, who have little to no experience with a collective-prioritizing mindset. Even within myself, I feel the seductive power and control of the individualist mentality. It's difficult, at times, to not revert to this way of thinking. It is so easy to leave when things get hard — and sometimes, we may actually need to! It's a balancing game, and we must listen to our intuition and take care of ourselves. But that said, I want to encourage you to find communities of Aliveness and commit to them, given how quick we normally are to go our own way.

CONCLUSION: OUR WHOLE LIFE

Frodo: I wish the ring had never come to me. I wish none of this had happened.

Gandalf: So do all who live to see such times, but that is not for them to decide. All we have to decide is what to do with the time that is given to us."

JRR Tolkien — *Lord of the Rings*

On this night, they say the veil between the living and the dead is thin. It's November 2, 2024, also known as Dia de los Muertos, a holiday that translates to Day of the Dead and is celebrated in Mexico and around the world. Coming on the heels of Halloween, Dia de los Muertos is a night for the spirits of the deceased to return and be merry, a colorful celebration of remembrance, music, Marigold flowers, and skeletal face paint.

And the Mission, a traditionally Mexican neighborhood in San Francisco, is *alive*. There are altars all around Potrero Del Sol Park, a lively musical procession down 24th St., and the streets are filled with people. It feels fitting that I'm writing the final chapter of this book on a day dedicated to the dead yet celebrated in such an alive way. It's an hour until midnight, and I can hear the music still going from the open window in my room; the visiting dead are, it seems, being treated to a good time.

It is never far from my mind that, at some point in the next 100 years, those visiting dead will include me and you. This reflection feeds my fire to be *alive*, to live this precious life to the fullest. As Shenryu Suzuki put it, "When you do something, you should do it with your whole body and mind. You should do it completely, like a good bonfire. You should not be a smoky fire. *You should burn yourself completely.*"

MY WAY FORWARD

In August 2023, when I was in Brooklyn for my *Jukai* retreat and ceremony, I was chatting with one of the residents there about his new job. He had recently finished his Clinical Pastoral Education (CPE) accreditation and was working as an interfaith chaplain at one of the largest hospitals in the area. As he described his work — providing spiritual care to patients dealing with illness and end-of-life — I was instantly intrigued. It sounded like a fascinating profession, and I could feel the charge that it lit inside me.

Just the next week, after I got back home to the Bay Area, a very close friend mentioned he was considering a yearlong training program in Buddhist chaplaincy. The program was not a full-time, accredited CPE, but instead was a way to explore the work and get trained to volunteer as a chaplain.

It was perfect — a way to take a first step. I applied as soon as I could. I've come to recognize this sort of synchronicity as one of the mystical ways Aliveness presents itself to us. When I wrapped up the program last year, I was clear that I didn't want to try to make it my livelihood, but I was (and still am) in love with how it's allowed me to volunteer as a chaplain at a local hospital. My chaplaincy training and work have become an integral part of how I live my Vow of Aliveness.

This story is a great example of how my Vow has taken the reins of my life. I don't have a neat little bow to put on my story as we close out our time together. I'm *choosing* to not figure it out with thoughts in my mind. Aliveness, as you know by now, doesn't work like that. What I do have is a direction — a clear sense of truth energy I'm following. I know the time and place where I will find this energy (now, in this body), and I have the resolve to keep going wherever it takes me. Staying in this journey of presence, inquiry, and charge is the only ask I have of my future, the only aim of my path.

THE PATH OF ALIVENESS

Living with Aliveness is both as natural as it gets and, given the reality of the default world, one of the most challenging paths possible. It's our birthright — literally what we're born with — but the default world systematically disconnects us from it through distraction, unworthiness, and endless validation-seeking. The reconnection process is paradoxically simple (just be present) and immensely challenging (in that it requires us to confront our deepest conditioning).

Aliveness has two sides. One is purposeful engagement — throwing ourselves into the projects, relationships, and causes that light us up inside. The other is spacious presence, a radical peace with whatever is happening right now. These aren't opposed but rather two faces of the same coin. Our most profound purpose flows from presence, and our presence deepens when we're engaged in what truly matters to us.

We can trust and follow our Inner World through a simple but powerful loop: getting *curious* about what's happening inside, bringing our attention into our *bodies, feeling* whatever arises, and *allowing* life to flow from there. As we practice this Loop of Aliveness, we learn to recognize charge — that unmistakable energy accompanying anything that has real meaning for us. This charge becomes our compass, navigating us toward what's truly alive.

But given the immense pull of the default world, *we need to treat this journey as a vow.* By giving it our commitment, it protects our minds and hearts from numbness and distraction. We live more and more alive, every day. As difficult as it is to feel our fear, grief, and the raw vulnerability of our beating heart, we find that this alternative is vastly superior to the life in which we're dead long before our chest stops thumping. The choice is stark: consumption, distraction, and dissociation – or Aliveness.

DOING IT TOGETHER

Finally, we can't do it alone. The default world is too powerful; its pull is too strong. We need regular rituals and practices that are mindful *and* embodied, and alternative spaces and communities that reflect our Aliveness back to us.

There's something bigger at play here, too — our individual journeys of Aliveness are intimately connected to collective transformation. The same forces deadening our individual lives are destroying our planet. Living our Aliveness isn't just about personal liberation — it's about being part of the change our world so desperately needs.

From wealth inequality to climate change to social systems like healthcare and education, in today's world, almost no one wins, and our future looks increasingly bleak. But I believe that if enough of us decide we want to be alive more than we want to maximize what we can take for ourselves, the big problems will work themselves out.

This decision starts with each one of us. It then builds into where we spend our time, what we buy, and who we hang out with. From there, it grows into the ways we think about our social systems and institutions: what their function is, who they serve, and how they operate. Aliveness offers us a startling clarity at every level of our civilization: personal, relational, societal, governmental, economic, and so on.

Even as the words flow from my fingertips, it seems impossible. And yet *we have no other way*, outside of increasingly capitalistic control that tries to squeeze the last few cents of profit out of dwindling resources and an ecologically dying planet.

In *Pleasure Activism,* adrienne maree brown writes: "I have seen, over and over, the connection between tuning in to what brings Aliveness into our systems and being able to access personal, relational and communal power. Conversely, I have seen how denying our full, complex selves—denying our Aliveness and our needs as living, sensual beings—increases the chance that we will be at odds with ourselves, our loved ones, our coworkers, and our neighbors on this planet."

The recent election only serves to clarify the urgent nature of our collective situation. Aliveness, then, is not just the compass pointing to our true north, but the burning directive for our lifetimes in this very specific moment in history. May we live it together.

OUR WHOLE LIFE

I wrote a poem for a dear friend who revels in long walks across San Francisco. During these walks, they reflect on their life. They replay things that happened and wonder about how they might show up with more self-confidence. They practice what they might say in certain situations to better support themselves.

The walks have been profound for them, opening up space for self-love and personal breakthroughs. They've had a chance to see the trance of unworthiness show up inside their self-talk, opening up a whole new relationship to themselves in the process.

They asked me to relate this process to this book and Aliveness as a whole. My primary answer was that I didn't know — only each of us can ascertain what Aliveness is for our specific being. Clearly, the walks seemed helpful for my friend, and I didn't want to interrupt something beneficial in any way.

Yet, I couldn't help but invoke a Zen perspective: any time we're using words to help ourselves feel better, we're constructing a brighter, shinier thought world. While this can be helpful in countless ways, if this sort of approach to life is our primary strategy, we're still in the realm of inauthenticity and the trance of unworthiness.

Self-love can express itself as words in our head, but it's fundamentally a feeling that arises spontaneously when we come into contact with our Inner World. Better self-talk can be immensely healing — and yet, it falls short of Aliveness. When we base our lives on stories we tell and re-tell ourselves, they demand certain actions and whole identities from us.

We stay a layer removed from the life happening right now. *That "right now" life* is the source of our Aliveness, and living it will always include stepping out of our ideas and into the unknown of this moment.

In writing the poem, I realized it was really for me and you, and that it was how I wanted to bid you farewell. Aliveness will always be risky, daunting, even terrifying — but what it offers us is our whole life.

Don't think so much
On your long walks
Through our fair city
Instead, feel the ground beneath you

This is no simple task
The ground has a reality
That cuts through your endless ideas
About who you are

You might be forced to feel
the way you pound your feet
You might be forced to feel
the truths in your heart

You might need
to move more slowly
You might need
to feel your pain

But I implore you because
The un-self-conscious life
Flows from that ground
Flows from your beating heart

The gratification
of your idea world
is a mirage of water
It does not quench thirst

One of these years
You'll realize what
you were chasing
Was validation, not life

Wanting validation is valid
It keeps us safe, in a way
But this safety is a fort
That keeps out our life

The impossible faith
I ask of you
Is to trust Aliveness
To stake your being on its truth

This truth, the feeling of the ground
Is not an obligation
But an experiment to see
What wisdom it speaks to you

To receive its power to
not just show you your darkness
But the light underneath
And how You've been avoiding it

This light won't always make you happy
It brings ecstasy and despair
But both will allow the flow of blood
to reach your limbs once again

This light asks us
To risk our whole heart
In return, it gives us
Our whole life

NOTE FROM THE AUTHOR

Hi there. Most of all, I want to thank you for reading. I've been writing in various forms for about five years and have been an avid reader since I was kid. The books I've read have shaped me so deeply, and I'm thrilled to be sharing my own work into the universe of written word. This thing we're doing – reading, sharing, writing, harmonizing our ideas and lessons — is one of my life's deepest joys. I decided to stick this note here because I want to tell you about where I'm at now, some ideas I'm passionate about working on, and how we can do that together.

I started to write this book for a lot of reasons: to share the process and underpinnings of the workshops/rituals I was hosting, to articulate a perspective of personal clarity, to make sense of my journey so far, and many more.

But along the way, I discovered this book's primary purpose: finding you. I want to share my work and life with like-spirited people. If you've read to this point, you are very clearly one of the people I want to meet.

If you're interested in being in touch, please reach out! I keep a blog on Substack where I share essays, poems, and photography that contemplate the intersections of Zen and my life. The QR code below (or directly navigating to https://ravimishra.substack.com) will take you to my blog, and if you reply to the email you get after signing up, it'll go straight to my inbox. You can also contact me via my website (https://ravimishra.com/).

I'd love if you subscribed to my blog. Building an audience on Substack makes it easier for me to choose to do a silly thing like take a year and write a book (which I very much want to do again, on subjects like masculinity, being Indian American, meditation, and more). Beyond that, if you're so moved, please rate the book on Amazon and Goodreads, as these help others discover my work. If you know of online journals, podcasts, communities, or anything else where people might be interested in this book or my work, I'd love to be connected. I'd be happy to send your organization a bunch of books and show up for a chat.

Aside from that, I do coaching and consulting in the realm of Product, strategy, rituals and processes, and, well, anything else you think I might be able to do for you or your organization. I also offer pay-what-you-feel energy healing done virtually or in-person (in a tradition similar to Reiki). If you're interested in working together in any of these capacities, say hi and let's chat.

Finally, I wanted to include a note that my teacher had upon reading a draft of this book. I've shared stories of peak meditative experiences, but most of the time, sitting in meditation is not like that. In fact, even labeling these "peak" is a mistake. There is no ideal that we're building towards in practice. It is best to have no expectation, what in Zen is called "no gaining idea," of what we might experience in meditation practice.

THE GOOD STUFF

Ok, now the good stuff. I want to share a couple project ideas that I've been tinkering with for a decade.

The first is in the realm of friend networks and social media. Even before big tech went MAGA, our online places of connection have grown pretty crappy. They harvest our attention and eyeballs for their own profit and don't actually nourish our relationships.

Toward the end of my time working on Awaken, Emmye and I created a pilot for a social game that we called Kindred. We put interested friend groups and couples into text message threads with a phone number we controlled. Every weekday, we'd send these threads a prompt: a check-in question, creative challenge, shared memory, or playful riddle.

The prompts were designed to catalyze connection, creativity, and authentic sharing. The people in our pilot group loved the sharing and conversations that came out of these prompts, and we were interested in exploring the idea further. But as we checked in with ourselves, we realized we didn't have the energy to start something new, and we put the idea on ice.

However, I continue to believe in the potential of messaging apps or social media that actually helps bring us closer together and encourages genuine sharing and connection.

Second, I've had a vision of what a movement could look like stuck in my head since Occupy. How we spend our money and time is of utmost importance within capitalism. The unthinking, habitual ways we do so can end up empowering the people and companies who work to deepen the death grip of the default world.

What inspired me then (and still speaks to me today) is some way of organizing and aligning businesses that, well, don't suck — that don't destroy the planet and are fueled by sustainable and ethical practices — under some sort of banner. I imagine it like a "fair trade" badge but across every industry, giving folks the ability to opt into an economic world in which what they consume supports economies and movements that are building a more just and sane world.

Businesses would pay reasonable salaries to employees and then donate most of their profits to social movements. The movement efforts would then support direct action towards things like a cleaner environment, more accessible and just social systems, and a more equitable wealth structure. Ideally, the businesses would work together, being customers of each other when possible and helping each other succeed.

There's a spirit of Occupy Wall Street and Burning Man baked into this whole thing. Each of us has unique talents and gifts, and ideally, this multifaceted movement would allow people to engage in whatever ways they're most passionate about — as entrepreneurs, organizers, or even simply as consumers. Certain cooperatively run businesses and organizations (co-ops) share this approach, and a few, like Mondragon in Spain, have grown to enormous scale (though, in our capitalism-obsessed country, its story is hardly known).

The companies we're customers of in the default world make tons of money — what if we put all of that power towards making change?

Anyway, I'd love to build these together. There are so many global challenges that we need to face if we are to make life on Earth sustainable – I hope we can spend these precious lives doing something about our collective situation in ways that make us feel alive.

If you're at all inspired, please be in touch! Again, thank you from the bottom of my heart for reading. I wish you care and joy on your journey of Aliveness.

Ravi

 instagram.com/rmishra
 linkedin.com/in/ravimishra

ACKNOWLEDGMENTS

To my family: Mummy and Papa, I am grateful far beyond words. You were my heroes growing up and remain that way today. Your selflessness, values, and courage are bottomless sources of inspiration. The way you've encouraged me to grow into the person I want to be is something I never take for granted. I love you so, so much. Henna, you're the best sis a brother could ask for. Baba, Amma, Nana, Nani, Chachas, Chachis, Masi, Mama, Mami, Bhuas, Foofas, and so many others — deepest of bows, and thank you for the cradle you collectively raised me in.

To my teachers: Hogen Sensei, bowing to you is an act with no start and no end. Rev. angel and Lama Rod, thank you for your teachings and guidance in a pivotal period of my life, and the ongoing wisdom you continue to bestow on me. Shugen Roshi, Hojin Sensei, Shoan Osho, and Gokan, you make my life come alive with your teachings and show me what it means to be a bodhisattva with your stewardship. ZMM family, it still boggles my brain how deeply you are all in my heart. What good fortune to have moved to State Street a decade ago.

Emmye: What a journey it's been from one email in 2018 to here. Obviously, this book simply would not have happened without you. But in a much more profound way, our collaborative relationship over these various projects has truly been one of the highlights of my life. Watching you learn, grow, make music (literally and metaphorically), and step more and more into your power has taught me so much about Aliveness. Thank you for your patience, kindness, and genius over these past seven (!) years.

Derek: Guide, mentor, friend, coach, and fellow traveler — from the very first time we met, your kindness has shocked me. From giving advice to a meditation app competitor to alchemizing every anxiety, confusion, and foolishness I bring your way, I cherish our time together. Deep bows brother.

Paul: You've been an inspiration on this writing journey — and even more importantly, a dear friend. Thank you for all the encouragement, answers, and advice. I am so, so grateful.

Silvi, Dom: Thank you so much for your contributions to this book (diagrams and cover, respectively). It's been lovely working together and getting to know you both.

Dan, Melissa, Hammersly, Brenna, Jenn, Brad, Hailey, Henna: Thank you for reading the various versions of this book — your feedback has deeply shaped it.

Gigi: Thank you for both your feedback and, more importantly, being a comrade-in-arms throughout this process.

Maya: This book started with that phone call the night before I got laid off, winding through the weirdness that is Las Vegas. I am eternally grateful for everything you've taught me.

Pranab, Maya P, Hokyu, Joy, Chrissie, and others: Thanks for reading my various things and continuously encouraging me to write. Your consistent support was a big reason I took the leap to begin writing this.

To my friends, family, anyone I may have forgotten, and really, everyone who read this book: Thank you.

APPENDIX 1: THE SEASONAL DEEP DIVE

During the deep dive, we ask where we want to direct our time and energy. Are we hustling on a meaningful project? Taking a breather and prioritizing rest? Is a relationship taking priority, whether with a romantic partner, a child we're welcoming into the world, or a parent or family member we're caring for? How can we chart a course ahead that honors where we are and what's important to us in this chapter of our life?

I call the rituals *seasonal* (rather than quarterly) to remind myself that life, like nature, has seasons, and I do them around the equinoxes and solstices. We're part of nature, and in aligning with the flow of nature's seasons, we can ask ourselves how the major building blocks in our lives fit in with the season we're moving into.

The deep dive is broken up into three distinct parts, moving from looking back and reflecting to gazing ahead and visioning:

1. Reflection — reviewing what's happened in the past quarter and landing in the present

2. Exploring — connecting with our Inner World and what's alive within us, allowing intuition to lead
3. Deciding — tangibly charting the course ahead

Before and after each section, we take a few minutes for a break and some sort of embodiment practice (meditation, dance, stretching, etc.). I answer the prompts and questions via journaling, but if you want to do it some other way (recording voice notes, out loud with others, etc.), that's great too. Let's take a closer look at each of these sections.

REFLECTION

You can mark the start of this ritual in any way you'd like. Maybe you want to light a candle, make some tea, or do some other rite of opening, and it's always a good idea to start with a few minutes of belly breathing as a way of coming into the body. It's not required, and for many, this sort of thing can be a little too woo-woo, but the deep dive is *an encounter with yourself*. It's an inherently sacred thing, and because we're usually so distracted and habitually skimming the surface of life, it can be helpful to mark the start of the ritual in an intentional way. Think of it as a signal to our Inner World, declaring we're open to its guidance.

After opening, we begin by reviewing what's happened in our lives. This is done both to consolidate lessons our past may be teaching us and as a way of letting go of what we might still be carrying and landing in our current time and place.

You can catalyze this process by looking through photos, calendars, journal entries, and other similar artifacts of what's gone on in your life. While taking in the material, tune into what emotions and thoughts arise. These reactions are important starting points for understanding how we felt and still feel about what's been happening in our lives.

This space of reviewing what happened creates a portal, of sorts, in which we can more deeply embody our feelings around what happened in our lives. We give our Inner World a chance to express things that might have gone unnoticed in the moment.

Finally, reflection builds our understanding of the *context* of our lives — the background emotional and metaphysical territory that we've been traversing. Sometimes, as we look back, we see trends in their totality — things like, "wow, this was a really happy time for me". Perhaps we're even able to identify some key causes (for example, "I spent a lot of time hiking the past few months").

After going through the process of review, select three of the following questions to guide and deepen your reflection on how the last quarter went. This isn't an intellectual choice — read the questions, feel what sparks, and just start journaling. If you're in doubt, pick the first three.

- What was most important? What were the major events? Accomplishments? What memories stand out?
- What didn't happen? What were you not able to accomplish?
- What are you most proud of?
- Who helped you along the way?
- Which places, people, activities, etc. felt energizing?
- Which things felt de-energizing, like an energy drain?
- What did you learn? How did you grow?

Next, we move on to identifying where we want to spend our time focusing: what 2-4 parts of our life are calling for our attention? You can choose from the list below, but ideally it's a starting point and you're able to hone in on the articulation of the parts of your life that matter most for you. For example, "family" might be something you want to focus on, but if you're really looking to give attention to your relationship with your children, name that as your focus area.

The point is to get specific and use this exercise of choosing to feel a sense of meaning and importance. It may happen that you realize you need to change one of the focus areas of your life halfway through the ritual — that's totally fine!

Here's the list we use:

- Social life and community
- Romantic relationships
- Family
- Contribution & Purpose
- Career
- Finances
- Passions & Hobbies
- Physical Health
- Emotional/Mental Health
- Creativity
- Spiritual life
- Anything else!

If you're doing this ritual with others (which is highly recommended, you can join me on Zoom if you'd like!), we end the reflection section with some sharing. Here are some questions you can use as conversation prompts, but feel free to share whatever is alive as you go through this process. Allow each person 3-5 minutes to answer whichever of these questions they'd like without interruption:

- Which Areas of Life feel most meaningful right now?
- What are you proud of from the past season/quarter?

- What else stood out from what happened over the
  past season?

Feel free to discuss and converse normally after everyone's had a chance to share for however long you'd like. We've reached the end of the Reflection section! Now, we'll move onto Exploring. Take a break, drink some water, and do some stretching or quiet breathing as you like.

EXPLORING

The Exploring section is about opening up ourselves to possibilities for what our Priorities might be. We'll spend some time in an open brainstorm, where we're just tapping into our Inner World and allowing it to express itself via journaling or dialogue. After this, we'll take a look at what we came up with and decide which vibes, goals, and identities we want to set as our priorities.

Vibes

Brainstorming vibes is pretty straightforward. Feeling into everything that happened, we let ourselves free-write an initial list of 10+ vibes, and then we go back and prune this list down based on what's resonating mostly deeply. There is truly no limit to what a "vibe" might be — it's a word that evokes meaning for *you*, pointing to an emotional, experiential, or spiritual context within which you want to be living.

Here's some examples from the last time I did a brainstorm: Unhurried, elemental, empathetic, spacious, still, connected, open, on point, slowness, edgy, peaceful, shifting, adventure, expansive, consistent in how I show up. They don't need to be one word — they can be a phrase or even a short sentence, like a mantra or affirmation you want to keep close.

You can use these instructions to guide the process, and remember to let the brainstorm process flow, writing down whatever comes up without self-judgment:

- What were the vibes or feeling tones that you would use to describe the last quarter? Write as many as you can.
- Of your list, what are you attracted to? Not so attracted to?
- What are the feelings or vibes that you want to bring into next quarter? Write down as many words or phrases as you'd like to describe these.
- Return to the words/phrases you wrote down during the last section and pick 3ish vibes you want to focus on cultivating during the coming quarter.

Next, we'll brainstorm some habits or intentional activities that we can use to support the Vibes we chose.

- What tends to get in the way of your vibes in your everyday life?
- Brainstorm 1-5 activities that can mitigate these things that get in the way, help cultivate your vibes, and/or protect your attention? Ex: taking a walk and getting ice cream, moving phone out of bedroom, etc.
- Do you want any of these activities to be done with others? Who? Ex: taking a regular walk with a partner or nearby friend can be a great new habit!

That's it! You'll have a chance to revisit all of this stuff at the end of the ritual, so take what you have now as good enough and move on. Share the vibes you chose and how they spark Aliveness with your friends if you're doing this with others, taking 3-5 minutes each as you did earlier.

Goals

The basic structure of how we set Goals is the same as Vibes: first brainstorming and then trimming the list down. First, for each life area you chose, free-flow brainstorm 3-5+ goals. Here are some prompts to get you started — you don't need to answer these, but they can help to inspire you if you're stuck:

- What's going well and what's the next step?
- What's happening that you don't like and want to change?
- Have any long-term dreams that you'd like to work towards?
- What habits would you like to start or stop?
- What can you definitely achieve? What feels like a risk?
- Think of a role model – what have they done that you find inspiring?

After you're done, we'll narrow down to the ones we want to choose:

Highlight the most inspiring goals — feel into what's meaningful for you

1. For each highlighted goal, write *why* it matters to you
2. If that "why" feels more important, see if it makes more sense to make the "why" the goal (i.e. if your goal was to run 20 miles a week and this is because you want to be in better physical shape, maybe you'll be more motivated by "Getting in shape" being the goal — or not, it's totally up to you!)
3. Keep narrowing until you have 3-6 goals, merging related goals as needed

4. What major steps do you need to accomplish each goal? Break down goals into subgoals if it makes sense to do so

5. If you're doing this with friends, take a few minutes and share your goals as we've done previously. After that, be sure to step away and do something embodying — shake it out, stretch, or sit and breathe.

Identity

This question of "who am I?" is at the core of Zen and many other spiritual traditions. So as you might have guessed, this section is my favorite. Everything we've done up until now a first draft from which we explore the deeper layers of what's going on inside of us. Put differently, I'm personally less concerned with what my vibes and goals are than I am with using them to understand and explore who I am — and who I want to be.

With that in mind, let's dive into identity. For this section, look over your vibes and goals and brainstorm a list of Identities you're living into, using the prompts below as you find helpful. Remember, start by just writing whatever comes up, and then narrow it down at the end.

Try completing the sentence "I am..."

- What sort of person would have the specific vibe or accomplish a specific goal you chose? For example, if a goal you set was to "Run 20 miles a week", you might answer "runner" or "athlete". Try saying "I am an athlete" and see how that feels.
- Who is a real person who embodies a vibe or has accomplished a goal you chose? How would you describe them?

- To close: Narrow down your list by reading through it and feeling which identities spark the most Aliveness/curiosity.

If there are "I am a..." statements that give you that palpable sense of charge, great. If not, maybe there are some still waiting to be discovered. "I am" statements can feel loaded, but remember that this whole thing is a trial — we're trying on an identity as part of an iterative, learning process. So just go with what feels good, and don't worry about being perfect.

Do one last round of sharing, then take a break, being sure to include a few minutes of embodied practice (stretching, walking, breathing, etc.).

DECIDING

At the end of the deep dive, we wrap each of these explorations into one simple document, called your Compass. Now that you've done all this juicy exploration, it's time to shrink it down into something that carries meaning and power for you — and something that can be easily revisited on a regular basis.

Write down your vibes, goals, and identities at the top. After that, write down any other takeaways that surprised you — anything you felt was noteworthy from this ritual. Personally, I just write my priorities (vibes, goals, and identities) and other takeaways on Post-It notes that I place around my desk and other frequented spaces. But if it inspires you, make it creative! Some people hand-draw a very artistic version of their Compass.

Summarizing onto the Compass makes it easy to read and re-read what you came up with. Ideally, you'll revisit it every week when you do your weekly planning. And personally, revisiting my Compass is all I commit to. More than accomplishing specific goals, what I want is to stay close to the energy of reflection and clarity that emerges during the deep dive, so that I can use it to orient me during my quarter.

However we use it, the Compass allows us to more easily insert our deeply felt priorities into our everyday lives. If you want the Google Doc that I use to capture my own compass, join my email list or email me, and I'd be happy to send them over.

While things can always change, the priorities we come up with during the deep dive ritual are meant to be our pillars for the upcoming quarter of a year (or until the next deep dive if you want to do them at a different interval). You'll use the priorities you came up to lay the groundwork for what you prioritize each week and day.

APPENDIX 2: THE DAILY STANDUP

All of the insights and aspirations from the seasonal deep dive come alive in a 15 minute standup I do each morning. These standups tie everything together, bringing our deep inner exploration into how we actually live. I do it with friends via Zoom — which is such a fun way to connect with people I love — but I also do it solo when my friends are unavailable. Most of the routine is done in silence, and during the last part, we unmute and share one thing about our days with each other.

The structure of these calls is always the same:

1. Start with 30 seconds of mindful breathing as a way of landing
2. Individually review what happened yesterday and our weekly goals, and make a list for what we want to get done today.
3. Designate one thing as the most important thing (MIT) for the day and list what else, if anything, you want to get done.

4. Select a vibe you want to bring to mind over the course of the day, whether it's your weekly vibe or otherwise.

5. Schedule time on your calendar for each thing you'd like to get done today, giving priority to getting the MIT done early if it feels right

6. Schedule time for your vibe, if applicable, and any other items of self care: meals, breaks, walks, workouts, meditation, etc.

7. Share one thing about your day with the crew you're doing it with

8. Breathe together for 30 seconds before closing out and starting your day

On Mondays, after doing some breathing, we'll start the calls with 4 more items to pave the way for the week:

1. Start by reading your Compass, grounding in the deeper intentions for this season

2. Set 3 weekly goals — things we want to get done (usually these are work-related)

3. If it helps, break those goals down into smaller chunks of work — this doesn't need to be 100% accurate, but it helps to know the major things to accomplish to complete a goal

4. Look over your list of vibes and select one of them (or something else) as your weekly vibe

One important note for all of this is to not change your daily and weekly goals and vibes during the week (unless it's absolutely needed). We spend so much time lost in cycles of evaluation and re-prioritization that we actually get a lot less done than we otherwise would (and stress ourselves out in the process). We'll have a chance to re-evaluate in the future

— during the week, the idea is to trust the goals we've picked on Monday and simply execute.

When my life is held by the deep dive and daily standup rituals, navigating the everyday gets easy and even magical. When I wake up on a random Thursday morning slightly groggy, all I have to do is make it to the standup and my day gets sorted out. I know that I've already been intentional about the big picture — the hard prioritization of what's really important. As such, I can relax in the container I've created and just pick up where I left off and plan my day — all while saying hi to some of my closest friends.

That's it! As always, take the pieces of this that work for you, and don't worry about the rest.